I0831997

Be Ooh La La

ACHIEVE YOUR GOALS AND TRANSFORM INTO YOUR BEST SELF

RAPHAEL POIROT

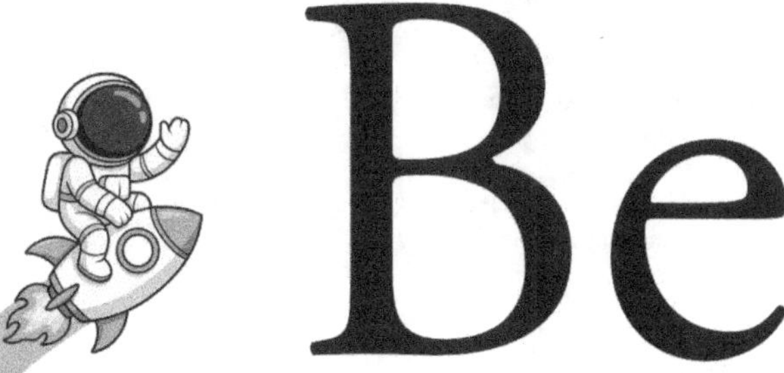

Be Ooh La La

ACHIEVE YOUR GOALS AND TRANSFORM INTO YOUR BEST SELF

RAPHAEL POIROT

Be Ooh La La: Achieve Your Goals and Transform into Your Best Self
Published by Altitude Press
Hawthorn Woods, IL, USA

This publication is designed to provide general guidance and information on personal growth and transformation. It is not intended as a substitute for professional advice. Readers are encouraged to seek personalized support from qualified professionals when necessary.

Disclaimer: The author and publisher make no guarantees about the outcomes resulting from the application of the ideas in this book. Every effort has been made to ensure the accuracy of the information herein at the time of publication. In the event you use any of the information in this book for yourself, the author and the publisher assume no responsibility for your actions.

To protect the privacy of others, certain names and details have been changed.

POIROT, RAPHAEL, Author
BE OOH LA LA
RAPHAEL POIROT

Library of Congress Control Number: 2025922334

ISBN: 979-8-9930841-0-7, 979-8-9930841-2-1 (paperback)
ISBN: 979-8-9930841-3-8 (hardcover)
ISBN: 979-8-9930841-1-4 (digital)

SELF-HELP / Personal Growth / Success
SELF-HELP / Motivational & Inspirational
BUSINESS & ECONOMICS / Personal Success

First Edition, October 2025
Cover and Interior Design by Katarina Naskovski
Edited by Ashley Emma, Abby-Eve Editorial, and Yoanna Stefanova
Publishing Consultant: Susie Schaefer (finishthebookpublishing.com)
Author Photo by Michael Delott

QUANTITY PURCHASES: Schools, companies, professional groups, clubs,
and other organizations may qualify for special terms when ordering quantities of this title.

For information, email: info@raphaelpoirot.com
www.raphaelpoirot.com

This book is printed in the United States of America.

For my wife, Amii, and my daughter, Lauren—
because you are, and will always be, my *Ooh La La*.

TABLE OF CONTENTS

INTRODUCTION

You're standing at the edge of something big.

Maybe it's a dream you've carried for years, a business idea, creative project, or even a new direction you can't stop thinking about. Or maybe it's something less defined, just a quiet knowing: *You're meant for more than this. You're meant to be Ooh La La!*

But every time you get close, doubt creeps in.

What if I'm not ready? What if I fail? What if I don't have what it takes?

So you pause. You play it safe. And "someday" stays just that, someday.

Well, this book is here to change that.

Imagine this: You're on the launchpad. Engines primed. Destination locked. The countdown ticks down as the ground shudders beneath you, energy thrumming in the air. Your heart pounds. This is the moment you've been working toward.

Everything is set. All systems are go. You feel the pressure of what lies ahead but also the ignition catching fire beneath you.

This is the moment before liftoff. The moment when you stop questioning and start moving.

Because launching into space or your boldest dreams takes more than a blueprint.

It requires a decision. A leap. A commitment to take that first irreversible step forward.

And that's precisely what this book will help you do.

Be Ooh La La is your flight manual, guiding you through your transformation journey.

Success isn't reserved for the lucky few. It's not a matter of being the smartest or the most connected; it's about preparation, mindset, and the courage to keep going. Inside these pages, you'll learn how to ignite your inner fire, silence the overthinking, and move from someday to right now.

Your mission?

To step into your full potential and live the life you were meant for, your own version of *Ooh La La*.

Ooh La La—More Than Just a Phrase

As a French person living and working internationally, I've heard it countless times: "Oh, you're French? *Ooh La La*!"

At first, I took it as a playful expression. But early in my career, my teams turned "*Ooh La La*" into a way to measure success. "How did I do? Is it *Ooh La La*?" they'd ask.

What began as a lighthearted phrase soon became a shared language for growth, high standards, and celebration. Over time, through my work in leadership, coaching, and change management, it evolved again, this time into something deeper: a framework for transformation.

I realized that personal and professional growth often unfolds in three distinct stages, which align perfectly with this simple phrase:

- *Ooh* – The beginning. You feel stuck, uncertain, or dissatisfied with where you are.
- *Ooh La* – The transition. You've started taking action, stepping outside your comfort zone, but challenges still feel overwhelming.
- *Ooh La La* – The breakthrough. Your hard work is paying off, momentum is building, and you're thriving.

This book is designed to help you move from "*Ooh*" to "*Ooh La La*"—guiding you in building the habits, mindset, and strategies needed to turn your goals into reality.

So, the next time you hear someone say, "*Ooh La La,*" know that it's more than a phrase; it's a state of being. And it's one you're about to reach.

Defining Success on Your Terms

Success isn't a formula, and it's certainly not one-size-fits-all. It's not about wealth, status, or achievements alone; it's about aligning your life with what truly matters to you.

Maybe your goal is to start a thriving business, publish a book, launch a passion project, or simply create more balance and fulfillment. Whatever it is, your personal definition of success is the only one that matters.

Take a moment: What does success look like for *you*?

Is your vision crystal clear, or are you still figuring it out?

Wherever you are on the path, this book will meet you there, helping you move from uncertainty to clarity, from dreaming to doing, from *Ooh* to *Ooh La La.*

Why I Wrote This Book

Over the past twenty-five years, I've led high-performing teams, coached entrepreneurs, and helped businesses navigate complex transformations. I've managed everything from small business operations to billion-dollar portfolios at a Fortune 50 company. I've worked alongside leaders scaling startups and others reinventing themselves completely.

Here's what I've learned:

The people who succeed aren't always the smartest, the richest, or the most connected.

They're the ones who take action. Who adapt. Who keep going.

I wrote this book for anyone ready to break free from doubt and step into their highest potential. Whether you're launching something new, scaling your success, or reinventing yourself, *Be Ooh La La* is your guide to getting there.

How to Use This Book

Think of this book as your flight manual for success. It's structured into three key phases, each essential to achieving lasting transformation:

- Part 1: Awareness – Igniting the Spark Within
  Every journey starts with awareness. In this section, you'll learn to recognize your intrinsic power, define your vision, and explore the importance of self-awareness as the foundation for your transformation.

- Part 2: Readiness – Preparing for Liftoff
  With your vision in place, it's time to craft your game plan. This section focuses on planning, preparing for obstacles, and building a support system to keep you on track.

- Part 3: Adoption – Lift Off into Action
  Finally, it's time to launch. This part is dedicated to taking decisive steps, adapting to challenges, and continuously moving forward toward your goals. It's where your dreams begin to materialize, and your life transforms.

Each chapter offers real-life stories, hands-on exercises, and reflection tools you can use right away, designed to meet you where you are and move with you as you grow. You won't be memorizing formulas or forcing a one-size-fits-all solution; instead, you'll explore a guided yet flexible process that helps you find your rhythm, your voice, and your version of success. This is a book you read and use.

Your Mission Starts Now

Right now, you have a choice.

You can keep doing what you've always done: waiting for the perfect moment, second-guessing yourself, putting your dreams on hold. Or you can make a different choice—you can start.

You don't have to have all the answers. You don't have to feel fully ready. You just have to take that first step. Because the moment you do, something incredible happens: momentum kicks in.

And once it does, nothing can stop you.

Throughout this book, we'll use the metaphor of a space mission to illustrate the journey of transformation. Just like astronauts meticulously prepare for liftoff, navigate the challenges of space, and adjust their course along the way, you too will embark on a mission, one that requires vision, preparation, and the courage to start.

Your goals are the planets you're reaching for. Your mindset and habits are the fuel that will power your journey. And along the way, you'll build the systems and strategies needed to keep your mission on course.

So, are you ready?

Turn the page. Your mission is about to begin.

CHAPTER 1

•

UNLOCK YOUR POTENTIAL

Before we dive into the three key phases of transformation—Awareness, Readiness, and Adoption—this chapter marks your official starting point. Think of it as your pre launch sequence: the pivotal moment where you recognize that something needs to change and begin shifting your mindset to make that change happen.

Transformation doesn't begin with external action; it starts with an internal decision, a realization that you are ready for something more. In this chapter, you'll see how even small moments of awareness can unlock your potential and set you on the path to *Ooh La La*.

Now, let's begin.

1. A STORY OF TRANSFORMATION

Meet Marie. On paper, she had it all: a stable corporate job, a solid income, and the respect of her colleagues. But beneath the surface, something was off.

Each morning, she slipped into the same routine. The work was fine, the paycheck dependable, but her days felt flat. Like she was running on autopilot. Deep down, Marie knew she wasn't living up to her full potential. She wanted more. More joy, purpose, and alignment between what she did and who she truly was.

For Marie, that passion was health and wellness. She loved helping friends and family improve their fitness and well-being. But turning that passion into a business? That felt risky. It was hard to let go of the safety of her job, the predictability of her life. Fear and possibility tugged at her in equal measure.

One ordinary evening, while taking a walk in the park to clear her mind, Marie encountered a scene that changed everything. A group of people exercising together, laughing, encouraging one another, and truly living in the moment. Something about the scene struck her. It wasn't just about exercise; it was connection, joy, and purpose in motion.

That moment stirred something in her. A forgotten part of herself. It was the wake-up call she didn't know she'd been waiting for.

That was the spark.

Marie decided to pursue her dream of starting a health coaching business. She didn't have it all figured out, but she didn't need to. She began learning, seeking advice, taking courses—each step pulling her closer to the life she envisioned.

Marie's journey can be divided into three distinct phases:

The "*Ooh*" Phase: Recognizing dissatisfaction—The wake-up call

At the outset, Marie was in what we call the "*Ooh*" phase—a state characterized by unfulfilled potential and a lingering sense of dissatisfaction. Like many of us in the "*Ooh*" phase, she felt a quiet dissatisfaction that something was missing but couldn't yet name it.

For Marie, the corporate world provided comfort but not fulfillment. She was merely going through the motions, her dreams buried beneath layers of routine and obligation.

The "*Ooh La*" Phase: Taking the first steps—The early action

As Marie began to act on her newfound inspiration, she entered the "*Ooh La*" phase. The first step toward change, a time filled with both excitement and nervousness, marks this stage. Marie attended workshops, studied business management, and sought advice from experienced professionals.

Progress was slow and often shadowed by self-doubt, but each small step laid a foundation for her bigger goal.

The "*Ooh La*" phase is important because it shows that change is possible, even if the results aren't yet dramatic.

The "*Ooh La La*" Phase: Realizing your potential—The breakthrough.

Eventually, Marie's persistent efforts began to bear fruit. Her first clients started to see positive changes, and her confidence grew with each success. Entering the "*Ooh La La*" phase, Marie not only transformed her business but also herself. She became more focused, resourceful, and resilient.

Her once-dormant passion had evolved into a thriving enterprise that positively influenced the lives of her clients.

Marie's transformation into the "*Ooh La La*" state is a testament to what's possible when you embrace change, overcome your fears, and commit wholeheartedly to your vision.

Have you ever had a moment like Marie's walk in the park? Maybe it wasn't in a park. Maybe it was a late-night thought, a conversation that stuck with you, or a growing sense that you're meant for more. If you've ever had that flicker of clarity, that whisper of "what if?" you've already taken your first step.

2. EMBRACING THE JOURNEY

Marie's story isn't solely about launching a successful health coaching business; it's about a profound personal transformation. Her transformation shows us that success is about the growth that occurs along the way.

We all carry untapped potential. The key is recognizing that discomfort is part of the process. Change is never easy, but it's how we grow into who we're meant to be.

You've stepped into the first stage of transformation—Unlock—and with it, the journey is already in motion.

There's no going back to autopilot. You've cracked the door open. What lies ahead is a complete roadmap for change.

This isn't guesswork. It's a clear, practical journey comprising eleven steps, mapped across the three phases introduced earlier: Awareness, Readiness, and Adoption.

Together, they form the *Ooh La La* Roadmap: your guide for navigating change with clarity and intention. Each chapter corresponds to one step, helping you build momentum one layer at a time. And throughout the book, you'll come back to the *Ooh* › *Ooh La* › *Ooh La La* Scale as a way to check in with yourself: where you are, what's shifting, and what's next.

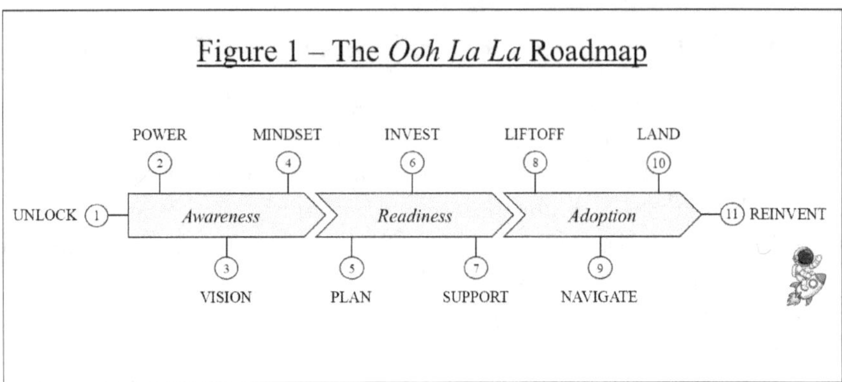

Figure 1 – The *Ooh La La* Roadmap

The tools themselves are drawn from three foundational disciplines that shape how transformation happens:

- *Change Management* gives you the structure to move forward with intention. It's about creating a clear path, anticipating obstacles, planning for momentum, and building sustainable progress.
- *Leadership* starts with self-leadership. It's the ability to act with clarity and courage, take ownership of your direction, and lead yourself even when the way forward feels uncertain.
- *Coaching* reminds us that growth doesn't happen in isolation. Seeking support, staying curious, and being open to feedback are all part of accelerating transformation.

These foundations are the engine behind the roadmap. You'll see them woven into the tools, prompts, stories, and strategies you'll use along the way.

At the end of each chapter, you'll pause to reflect, checking in on your place within the roadmap and what comes next. These moments are here to keep you grounded, aligned, and in motion.

You're in it now.

Enjoy the ride.

3. YOUR INVITATION TO TRANSFORM

Marie's story might sound familiar. Not because everyone wants to become a health coach but because her deeper journey—the tension she felt, the quiet unrest, the slow awakening—mirrors what so many of us experience when we know we're meant for more.

Maybe you're feeling it, too. That pull toward something that hasn't fully taken shape yet. It's not always loud. Sometimes it's just a whisper. A growing discomfort with staying where you are.

A flicker of inspiration that won't go away.

A question you can't shake: *What if there's more than this?*

That's how it started for me.

For years, I carried an idea that didn't quite have a name. I'd hear the phrase "*Ooh La La*" and smile; it was playful, familiar. However, over time, I noticed something. This simple expression would appear in moments of energy, growth, and transformation. I'd hear it after a breakthrough in coaching, pitching a bold idea, or celebrating a small but powerful step. It meant something more.

Meanwhile, in the background, I had built a toolkit over the years: frameworks from change management, strategies from leadership development, insights from coaching, and hundreds of stories from real-life transformations. I knew these tools worked. I had seen them change teams, lives, and futures. But there was a disconnect. I had all the ingredients, yet I wasn't entirely using them to build what I knew I could.

That was my Unlock.

It didn't come with a bang. It came more like a click. A subtle but undeniable moment when I realized: I don't need another degree, a better idea, or a perfect plan. I already have what I need to start. I just hadn't committed yet.

You might be in that space right now, holding onto a passion, a desire, or a vision that's still taking shape. That's okay. Unlocking your potential doesn't require perfect clarity. It requires a willingness to stop circling the launchpad and take one step forward.

So, let's make this real.

Here's how to find your own Unlock moment and act on it.

TRY THIS:

1. Identify Your "Ooh" Moment

Where do you feel a disconnect between who you are and what you're doing? Maybe it's a project you keep dreaming about, a shift you feel ready for, or simply a sense that something in your life is out of alignment.
The "*Ooh*" phase is uncomfortable, but it's also a signpost. It means your awareness is waking up.

2. Define One Small Unlock

No one's saying you need to quit your job or plan your whole future right now. The shift starts with something smaller, a single choice that nudges you forward. So, what's one action you could take today to explore what's next?

- Write down an idea you've been carrying
- Send a message to someone who inspires you
- Research something that excites you
- Journal for five minutes about the change you crave

3. Commit to It

Don't wait for the timing to be perfect. It never is.
Take action within the next 24 hours to create forward momentum.
Write it down. Say it out loud. Tell a friend. Or better yet, just do it now.

That's how transformation begins. Not with the whole plan but with a flicker of action. A shift in your energy. A willingness to move from thinking to doing. Momentum.

You don't need to have it all figured out; that's what the rest of this journey is for. What matters most right now is your decision to keep going. To explore what's possible instead of staying safe in the known.

You've entered the Unlock phase, and that's no small thing. From this point on, the transformation becomes more tangible. With each chapter, you'll gain more clarity, more momentum, and more confidence to keep building.

We just got a glimpse of what awareness might feel like. Now, let's swing the door wide open. In this next phase, you'll tap into the internal fire that fuels your transformation.

You'll uncover the power that's already within you and learn how to use it to shape your future with purpose.

But for now, celebrate this:
You've taken the first step.
You've honored the nudge.
You've said yes to something more.
Your next step is waiting.

OOH LA LA HIGHLIGHTS

STEP 1: UNLOCK YOUR POTENTIAL

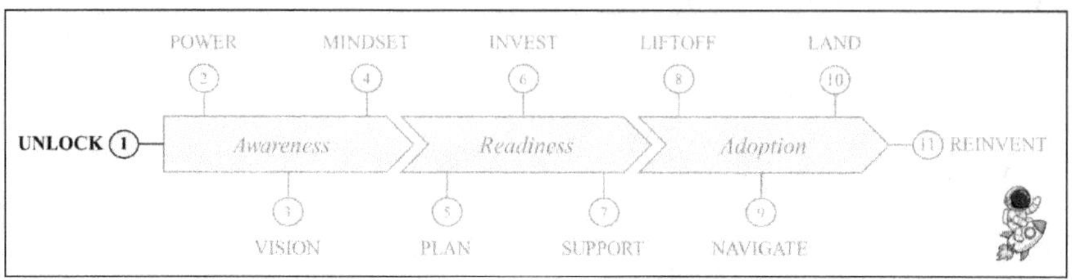

MISSION BRIEF

Unlocking your potential starts with a single internal decision: to stop settling and say yes to what's calling you forward. This first step is about acknowledging that you're ready for change, even if the whole picture isn't clear yet.

CRITICAL SYSTEM ANALYSIS

- Transformation begins with awareness. The "*Ooh*" phase, where something feels off—it is not failure; it's fuel. It's the moment you realize you're meant for more.
- Your journey follows a proven roadmap. The *Ooh La La* Roadmap includes eleven steps across three phases: Awareness, Readiness, and Adoption.
- Three essential forces power your transformation:
  - Change Management gives your growth structure and direction.
  - Leadership begins within. When you take ownership of your decisions, goals, and growth, you lead your transformation.
  - Coaching accelerates progress. Seeking guidance, feedback, and support.
- The *Ooh La La* Scale of Transformation:
  - ***Ooh*** Phase: The wake-up call. Something isn't right: You feel stuck, misaligned, or unfulfilled.
  - ***Ooh La*** Phase: The early action. You start exploring, learning, and

building momentum.

- ***Ooh La La*** Phase: The breakthrough. The moment your potential gains momentum, you experience purpose, confidence, and clarity.

PILOT'S REFLECTION

1. What is your "*Ooh*" moment? Where do you feel dissatisfaction or a call for change in your life?
2. What small action can you take today to start your transformation?
3. Who can support you? What mentors, coaches, or communities could guide you on this journey? Who do you already have access to?

NEXT COORDINATES

You're now in motion. Step 1—Unlock—is complete. As we enter Part I: Awareness, you'll uncover your inner power and define the direction that will fuel your transformation.

PART I

•

Awareness

Igniting the Spark Within

CHAPTER 2

•

THE POWER WITHIN YOU

"You were born with wings. Then why prefer to crawl through life?"
– Rumi

If Chapter 1 helped you awaken the idea that something greater is possible, this next chapter is where we begin powering up the systems that will take you there. The upcoming pages will help you tap into your inner strength, clarify your power, and give you the tools to launch with intention.

1. FUELING THE FIRE WITHIN

Let's go back to us standing on that launchpad, staring up at the vastness of space, the unknown calling to you, full of possibilities. Your spacecraft is ready, the engines humming with potential. But something holds you back, like gravity keeping you tethered to the ground. Maybe it's doubt, fear, past failures, or the weight of expectations.

Your transformation is on the other side of liftoff. You just have to trust in your power to launch. Take a deep breath. Close your eyes if you need to. Feel the strength that's already inside you and let that be the force that carries you forward.

From the moment we're born, we're astronauts in training; curious, fearless, and eager to explore. But as life unfolds, gravity in the form of doubt, insecurity, and routine begins to pull us down. We forget that we were born to soar. Instead of preparing for liftoff, we settle for what's comfortable.

But the difference between staying grounded and soaring into *Ooh La La* territory is awareness; awareness of what's holding you back, what's possible beyond your comfort zone, and the power you already carry within you.

You already have the wings and the power. The only question is: *Are you ready to step into the cockpit and take control of your journey?*

Understanding Your Intrinsic Power

Have you ever considered the limitless power that already exists within you? This intrinsic strength is your ultimate fuel source; it's what propels you forward, keeps you resilient in the face of setbacks, and drives you toward success.

Throughout history, great thinkers have recognized this power:

Marcus Aurelius: *"You have power over your mind, not outside events. Realize this, and you will find strength."*

Epictetus: *"It's not what happens to you, but how you react to it that matters."*

Emerson: *"What lies behind us and what lies before us are tiny matters compared to what lies within us."*

Nietzsche: *"He who has a why to live can bear almost any how."*

Lao Tzu: *"Mastering others is strength. Mastering yourself is true power."*

These insights remind us that true power isn't found out there but rather within. It's not about controlling circumstances but mastering ourselves.

The Building Blocks of Intrinsic Power

Just as no rocket launch can occur without a well-engineered system, your journey to *Ooh La La* success requires the right internal components working in harmony.

Here's your launch system:

Figure 2 – Building Blocks of Inner Power

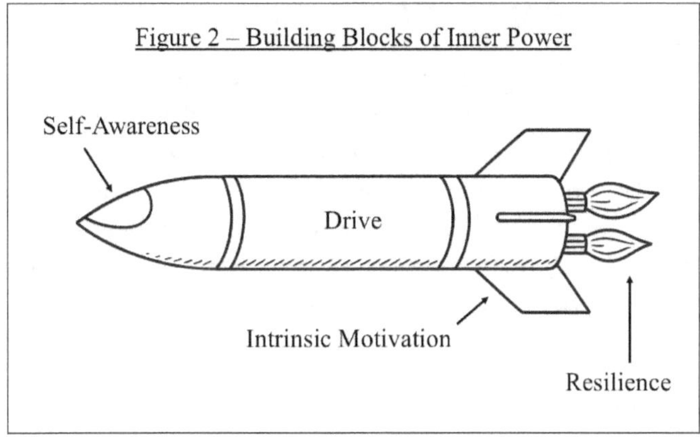

- *Self-Awareness: The Cockpit*
  This is your command center. Regularly check in: What are your strengths? Your values? What truly matters? Self-awareness sharpens your clarity, so you steer with purpose, not drift aimlessly.
- *Drive: The Fuel Tank and Engine*
  This is your internal energy source: the confidence, conviction, and courage to move forward. When guided by self-awareness, your drive becomes focused fuel instead of scattered effort.
- *Resilience: The Boosters*
  Setbacks are part of every journey. Resilience gives you the strength to rise again. It's your belief in yourself when doubt and challenges try to pull you down.
- *Intrinsic Motivation: The Navigation System*
  Your *why* is your compass. Unlike external rewards, intrinsic motivation is fueled by purpose. It keeps you aligned and moving through the difficult parts because you love the journey itself.

Your journey to *Ooh La La* doesn't start with some external permission slip. It starts the moment you recognize that you already have what it takes to launch.

The next step is learning how to tap into your power, strengthen it, and use it intentionally. Let's explore how you can discover and activate your power to move yourself forward.

2. DISCOVER AND TAP INTO YOUR INNER POWER

Sometimes, recognizing our power requires a defining moment, one that shakes us out of our routine and makes us see ourselves in a new light. Here's mine:

With a degree in engineering and business, I envisioned a corporate career marked by strategy, decision-making, and solving complex problems. But life had other plans. Early on, I found myself working the late shift at a retail drugstore in suburban Chicago, a far cry from the future I'd envisioned. I was managing inventory, assisting customers, and adjusting to the rhythms of retail and pharmacy work, wondering how it all fit into the bigger picture.

That's where I met Michelle, the store manager. She led with quiet authority. She didn't have to demand respect; she earned it naturally. Her team felt seen and valued. Customers were cared for. The store ran like clockwork.

I paid attention. I observed how she encouraged her team, navigated challenges, and fostered a culture of loyalty and high performance. Without realizing it, I was learning more than any business textbook had ever taught me.

At the time, I regularly worked the evening shift. If you've ever worked in retail, you know that the night shift is where many start. About a month into my time at the store, I was settling into my routine. One evening, as Michelle prepared to leave at her usual time, we went over the key tasks for the night. She purchased a few household items, gave a quick farewell, and walked out.

Ten minutes later, she returned.

I was in the office, updating inventory on the computer, when she walked in. She paused at the door and, in a simple but powerful moment, said something like: *"Raphael, I wanted to tell you; you're doing an excellent job. You have real leadership potential. I see the way you organize the team, how you treat people, and the consistently high quality of work you deliver. You have something special."*

I don't remember her exact words, but I remember exactly how they made me feel. It was an *Ooh La La* moment, one of those rare instances when someone sees something in you before you see it in yourself.

It flipped a switch inside me. I'd never thought of leadership or coaching as strengths. But here was someone I respected, telling me I had potential.

That short conversation changed everything. I realized that leadership and coaching, helping people achieve their goals, was something I naturally embodied. That realization shaped every step of my career. From that moment forward, I sought ways to develop my leadership skills, to inspire and grow others, and to tap into my full potential.

That's the thing about inner power, it's already there. Sometimes, it takes just one moment, insight, or one person's belief in you to help you recognize it.

Your Inner Power Is Already Within You—Here's How to Find It

Discovering your inner power is like prepping for launch. Astronauts undergo rigorous training to understand their strengths, and you can do the same through intentional self-discovery.

Here's how.

1. **Run a Self-Diagnosis: Reflect on What Energizes You**
   What makes time fly, what challenges excite rather than drain you? These moments reveal your strengths.
   Example: Do you come alive designing visuals, coaching breakthroughs, brainstorming ideas, writing, or performing?

2. **Consult Mission Control: Ask for Feedback**
   We often miss what's obvious to others. Ask colleagues, mentors, or friends what strengths they see in you.
   Example: A friend might say, "You simplify complex ideas so clearly," or "You make people feel heard," a sign of strong teaching, coaching, or storytelling ability.

3. **Explore Uncharted Territory: Try Something New**
   Growth lives outside your comfort zone. Take on new roles, join a group, or learn a new skill.
   Example: Trying out a podcast, teaching a workshop, launching a side hustle, or submitting your artwork might surface new creative or leadership talents.

4. **Review Past Missions: Reflect on Wins**
   Think about times you felt proud. What were you doing? What skills were at play?
   Example: Proud of organizing a gallery show, publishing a piece, coaching a client to success, or facilitating a team session? You might be naturally skilled in communication, leadership, or providing support.

5. **Keep a Flight Log: Write It Down**
   Journaling (or even listing achievements) can reveal patterns in what energizes and fulfills you.
   Example: If you repeatedly enjoy helping others grow, building new things from scratch, or turning ideas into finished work, that's a sign of coaching, entrepreneurship, or creative drive.

6. **Visualize Your Best Self: Picture Future You**
   Who are you when you're at your best? What do you do daily? How

do you lead, speak, or serve?
Example: If you see yourself writing books, hosting a retreat, leading a team, painting full-time, or launching a mission-driven brand, start embodying those actions today, even in small ways.

7. **Use Data: Take an Assessment**
Sometimes your greatest strengths feel too "obvious" to notice. Tools like StrengthsFinder, DISC, or 16Personalities offer fresh insights and language to describe what you're naturally great at.
Example: A client once discovered through an assessment that her direct communication style was driven by a strength in developing others. What her team saw as tough feedback was her deep care for their growth. That shift in awareness transformed both her leadership and her team dynamics.

Fueling Your Journey Forward

Inner power is already within you, waiting to be uncovered. And once you do, it becomes the fuel behind clear, confident action.

You don't need the whole map. You just need to trust the pull of where you're meant to go next. Whether it confirms your current path or reveals a new one, you'll know which way to go.

That single conversation with Michelle didn't immediately change my career, but it planted a seed, showing me I had something valuable to develop. That seed grew into a leadership philosophy shaping my mission to help others reach their potential.

And I remember the feeling.

It wasn't dramatic, but it was powerful. A spark in my chest. That sudden rush of clarity mixed with excitement, like my gut was saying, *"Pay attention."* I felt something shift. My mind started connecting dots I hadn't seen before. It was energizing. A little breathtaking. That quiet but certain feeling of, *"This matters."*

That was an *Ooh La La* moment.

Your defining moment might be waiting just around the corner. Or maybe, you've already experienced it but haven't fully recognized it yet.

Pause and think back to moments you felt *Ooh La La*: alive, capable, and in your element. Not just what you want to do but *who you're meant to become.*

In the next section, we'll explore why inner power isn't just nice to have, it's essential for the journey ahead!

3: YOUR INNER POWER IS KEY TO YOUR JOURNEY

No matter what you're building, a career, a calling, a creative life, your progress depends on something deeper than strategy: it depends on you. Your inner power fuels everything. It's what helps you move forward when things get hard, stay focused when the path gets messy, and make decisions that feel right.

Without it, you risk getting stuck in doubt, hesitation, or trying to live up to someone else's expectations. But when that power is activated, you stop waiting for permission and start building momentum.

Let's look at three ways your inner power makes a difference in your *Ooh La La* journey:

You Trust Yourself

Every transformation begins with a moment of doubt, the quiet question: *Can I do this?* That's where self-trust comes in, believing in your ability to figure it out, even when the path isn't clear.

Think of *The Matrix* (1999). At first, Neo doesn't believe he's The One. He doubts himself, questions his potential, and resists his calling. But then, he's beginning to believe, and everything shifts; he stops waiting for permission and trusts his power. Suddenly, the rules no longer apply. He defies gravity and becomes invincible.

Your journey is not different. Until you believe in yourself, you stay stuck, like Neo before the leap. The real battle is in your mind. And the moment you claim your power, everything begins to change.

Now ask yourself:

- What beliefs are keeping you stuck?
- What might happen if you let them go?

Like Neo, you have a choice: stay in the illusion of limits, or step into your power.

You Take the Lead

It's tempting to wait:

- *"I'll go for it when I have more time."*
- *"I'll start when I feel ready."*
- *"I'll leap when the timing is perfect."*

But the perfect moment never comes. You must create it. The people who achieve fundamental transformation don't wait for permission; they take ownership and move forward, even when it's messy or uncertain.

That's what Marie did. She loved health and wellness, but fear kept her in a job that no longer inspired her. She kept waiting, telling herself the timing wasn't right.

Everything changed the moment she took ownership of her future. That moment in the park, watching people living in alignment with their passion, made her realize she had a choice:

She could stay in her routine, playing it safe, or she could take the first step toward building the life she truly wanted.

Marie didn't know exactly how her journey would unfold, but she took ownership of her future. And that decision changed everything.

Now ask yourself:

- Where have you been waiting instead of leading?
- What's one decision you can make today to reclaim the driver's seat?

You Stay True to Yourself

One of the biggest traps? Chasing success that doesn't belong to you. It's easy to pursue goals that look good on paper but feel empty inside.

Authentic success should be about building a life that reflects who you truly are.

This ties to one of my favorite quotes from Oscar Wilde: *"Be yourself; everyone else is already taken."* If you don't define success for yourself, you might end up climbing a ladder leaning against the wrong wall.

That's why knowing your inner power means knowing your values, passions, and principles.

Marie's shift wasn't just about changing careers; it was about realignment. She defined success on her terms:

- Build community health programs that empower others
- Stay open to innovation and learning in wellness

- Lead with integrity and authenticity

With those values as her compass, her choices became clearer and more meaningful.

Ask yourself:

- What do you stand for?
- Are you living in alignment with your values, or someone else's version of success?

Your Inner Power is Your Edge

So, why does inner power matter?

✓ It helps you *trust yourself*, even when the next step feels uncertain.

✓ It gives you the courage to *take the lead*, instead of waiting for perfect timing.

✓ And it keeps you grounded—to *stay true to yourself*, even when others expect you to follow their path.

You don't have to wait for someone to choose you. You don't need all the answers.

You just need to begin by trusting the strength that's already within you.

Like Neo, the power's been there all along. The real question is: Will you claim it?

Next, we harness that inner power and transform it into clarity.

You'll define your vision, set meaningful goals, and shape success your way.

Your journey is about to accelerate. Let's set the course.

OOH LA LA HIGHLIGHTS

STEP 2: THE POWER WITHIN YOU

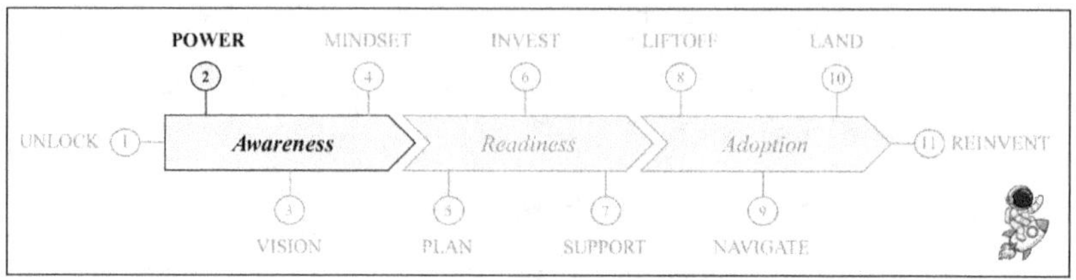

MISSION BRIEF

Your inner power is already within you; it's the fuel behind clarity, confidence, and momentum. When you learn to trust it, lead with it, and align your choices with it, transformation becomes not just possible but inevitable.

CRITICAL SYSTEM ANALYSIS

- The building blocks of inner power work together as a complete internal system:
    - Self-awareness is your cockpit, giving you clarity on who you are and where you're headed.
    - Drive is your fuel tank and engine, driving confidence, conviction, and courage to build momentum.
    - Resilience is your booster, pushing you through challenges and setbacks.
    - Intrinsic Motivation is your navigation system, keeping you aligned with your why.
- You can activate inner power through intentional reflection and action:
    - Look inward: Reflect on moments of pride, passion, and purpose.
    - Seek feedback: Let others reveal the strengths you may not see.
    - Step outside your comfort zone: Growth reveals hidden potential.
- Inner power matters for the journey ahead:

- It gives you the confidence to move forward, even in uncertainty.
- It shifts you from waiting to leading, from hesitation to momentum.
- It ensures your growth is rooted in who you are, not who you think you're supposed to be.

PILOT'S REFLECTION

1. What strengths or experiences have shaped your journey so far?
2. How can you begin using your inner power more intentionally?
3. What small action can you take today to trust in your abilities and move forward?

NEXT COORDINATES

Time to chart your mission. In the next chapter, we'll map your vision and set a clear course for your journey

CHAPTER 3

•

DEFINE A CLEAR VISION

1: THE ABC OF GOAL DEFINITION

"If you don't know where you are going, any road will get you there."
– Alice in Wonderland

Early on, Marie had taken bold steps toward her dream of building a wellness business, pouring her energy into every opportunity she could find. She attended workshops, networked with other entrepreneurs, and read every book she could get her hands on. On the surface, she was doing all the right things.

But something felt off.

Despite all her hard work, Marie often felt stuck, busy, yes, but unsure if she was truly moving forward. The harder she pushed, the more it seemed like she was running in circles.

One evening, during a conversation with her mentor, a simple question stopped her in her tracks:

"What exactly do you want?"

Marie hesitated. She knew she wanted to help people live healthier lives, but how? Was she building a coaching practice? Launching a wellness retreat? Creating an online platform?

She didn't have a clear answer. And in that moment, she realized why everything felt so unsettled. It wasn't a lack of effort; it was uncertainty about her direction.

Just like astronauts don't launch without a mission, you need a clear vision before you can truly take off.

That's where the ABC Model comes in.

The ABC Model

In coaching, we use a straightforward yet powerful framework to clarify goals, where:

- *Point A* is your current reality—where you are now. This step involves candidly assessing your strengths, weaknesses, opportunities, and threats. By being brutally honest about your present situation, you avoid making assumptions and gain a true understanding of your starting point.
- *Point B* is your destination—the vision of where you want to go and what you aspire to achieve. It's the life you dream of, filled with purpose and fulfillment. By clearly defining this future, you create a motivating and emotional connection to your goals, guiding your actions and decisions toward your success.
- *Point C* stands for Constraints and potential obstacles you may encounter (e.g., time, resources, knowledge). Identifying these constraints helps you formulate a specific plan to overcome them.

This framework helps you define your direction and identify the gap between where you are and where you want to be.

Think of it this way:

Point A → Point B = Your transformation.

Point C = The conditions that shape the path, both the roadblocks and the boosters.

For now, we'll focus on Points A and B—where you are and where you want to go.

We'll dive into Point C—your potential constraints and roadblocks in the next part, *Readiness*.

That's when we'll look at what might get in your way and how to plan for it.

First, let's clarify your destination and where you stand today.

Figure 3 – Your Journey Ahead

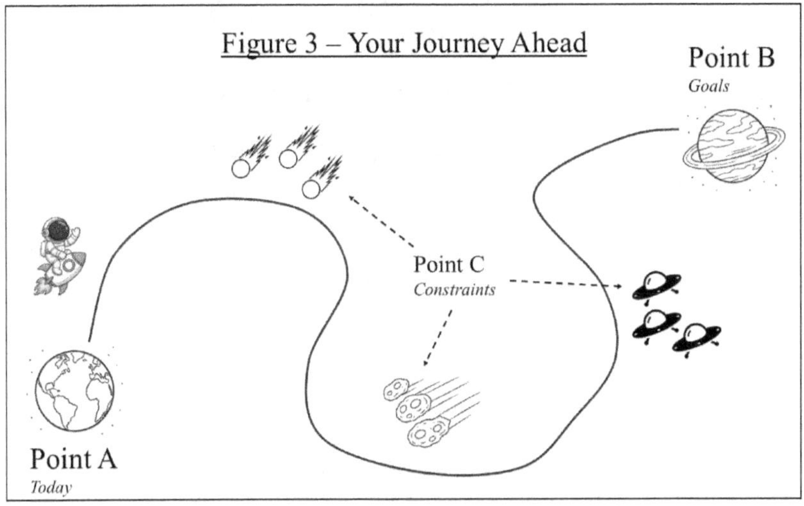

Why Knowing Your Destination is the First Step to Success

Stephen R. Covey, in *The 7 Habits of Highly Effective People*, wisely said, "Begin with the end in mind."

If you don't know where you're headed, it's easy to get lost. Many people work tirelessly toward success only to realize, years later, that they were climbing the wrong ladder. Without a clear vision, you risk chasing goals that don't truly fulfill you.

Defining your Point B gives your effort meaning. It ensures that each step you take moves you toward a future you genuinely want.

For Marie, that question: *"What exactly do you want?"* marked a turning point. Up until then, she had been moving with energy but without direction. Something needed to shift.

Ooh La La Tip: Using the ABC Model, I like to start with Point B as it allows you to dream big and focus on your ultimate goals without being constrained by current limitations or obstacles.

So, let's do just that in the next section, focusing on your Point B—your ultimate destination. What does success look like for you? What kind of life or career are you striving for?

Once that is clear, we'll assess Point A, your current reality, so we can bridge the gap between the two.

Now is the time to take control of your path and move with purpose toward the life you truly want.

2: POINT B - DEFINING YOUR VISION AND GOALS

Marie's Moment of Clarity: The Power of a Clear Vision

The question lingered in Marie's mind long after the conversation ended. *"What exactly do you want?"*

It echoed as she walked home, as she got ready for bed, even as she tried to sleep. She tossed and turned, restless because she cared so much, and yet, she couldn't quite see the shape of what she was building.

That night, she realized something important: she had been chasing movement, not meaning.

The next morning, with hardly any sleep, Marie made her way to a quiet café near her apartment. She ordered some tea and tucked herself into a window seat, journal in hand. The city was just waking up, but inside, her thoughts were already wide awake.

She started writing, curious to come up with some answers that resonate with her:

Why am I doing this? What does success feel like—not just for me but for the people I want to serve?

Slowly, the noise began to clear. She stopped thinking in disconnected tasks and started picturing lives, real people walking through her doors and leaving more confident, healthier, and connected. She imagined a warm, inviting space filled with energy, support, and transformation. Not just a service but a community.

For the first time, she could see it. Not in polished business terms but in feeling, in impact, in purpose.

Her vision was coming into focus.

Your Vision Matters

Astronauts don't launch without a destination, and neither should you. Without a clear vision, it's easy to get distracted, stuck, or burned out. But when you know where you're going, your choices align, your energy is focused, and even setbacks become part of the journey.

Your vision provides:

- Direction: A clear endpoint that helps you focus your time and energy.
- Purpose: A deep sense of motivation that sustains you through challenges.
- Decision Clarity: A framework for making choices that align with your long-term goals.

Think of your vision as a powerful declaration of where you are headed and why it matters. The clearer and more inspiring it is, the stronger your drive to pursue it.

Ooh La La Tip: Make Your Vision Real

A vision is not just an abstract idea; it should feel vivid and personal, something you can see, feel, and step into.

Ask yourself:

- What does my ideal future look like?
  - Where am I?
  - Who am I surrounded by?
  - What am I working on or building?
- How do I want to feel every day?
  - Energized? Free? Accomplished? Inspired?
- What impact do I want to make?
  - Who will benefit from my work?
  - What lasting difference do I want to leave behind?

A powerful vision is an experience in your mind that precedes its realization as reality.

EXERCISE: DESIGNING YOUR FUTURE LIKE AN ARCHITECT – THE 4-STEP METHOD

1. Sketch the Foundation: Identify your non-negotiables, the core pillars on which your future must stand.
2. Outline the Big Picture: Visualize the major elements of your life: career, relationships, lifestyle, achievements.
3. Add the Details: Fill in vivid specifics that make your vision feel alive.
4. Step Inside Your Vision: Immerse yourself in the future you've created and feel what it's like to live there.

Now, let's try it…

Imagine you're standing on a wide, open plot of land. The air is crisp, full of possibility. In your hands is a roll of pristine blueprints, not for a house but for the life you're about to build.

You crouch down, sketching the first lines. These are your foundations, the unshakable elements that will hold everything up. Maybe it's the freedom to choose your hours, the joy of meaningful work, the security of financial stability, or the warmth of close relationships. Without these, nothing else will feel steady.

Then, you step back and begin to outline the whole shape. Is your future expansive, full of open spaces for adventure? Or cozy, full of quiet corners for creativity and connection? As you draw, you're not just thinking of walls and windows; you're sketching your career, your relationships, your daily rituals, the milestones you'll celebrate.

Next come the details, and this is where the magic happens. You walk through the imagined rooms of your life:

- The morning light spilling over your breakfast table—where is that table?
- The people you work with—what energy do they bring?
- The conversations you have each day—what ideas do they spark?
- The victories that make you proud—what do they look like?

Finally, you put down your pencil and step right into the vision you've drawn. You can hear the echo of laughter in the hallways, feel the sun warming your face, and taste the satisfaction of living on purpose. Every detail breathes life into the picture.

This blueprint is alive. Like any great design, it will evolve as you do. But now you have a shape, a place, a vivid vision to guide you forward.

Crafting Your Vision Statement

Once you've walked through the vision of your future, it's time to give it a voice.

This is where you translate what you've seen into words; a vision statement that becomes your compass. Think of it as your personal mission patch, stitched onto your jacket for every adventure ahead. It's the reminder of where you're headed, especially on the days when the trail disappears into fog.

A good vision statement does more than list what you want. It sharpens your direction, connects you to your deepest "why," and quietly asks you, whenever a new choice appears: *"Does this align with the life I'm building?"* It keeps you anchored in your own path, not swept along by someone else's.

Your vision statement is your North Star. When life gets noisy or uncertain, it's what you can return to for clarity, courage, and momentum. But for it to guide you, it has to live in your mind and your heart.

The strongest vision statements are short enough to remember without effort, yet powerful enough to shift your mood when you say them out loud. They carry emotion; the kind that makes your chest expand and your pulse quicken. And they are clear: pointing you forward without locking you into a rigid map.

You'll know you've found yours when it feels like both a spark to set things in motion and a steady flame to guide you along the journey.

Marie's Vision Statement

After reflecting deeply on what she wanted to create, Marie translated her vision into these words:

"To create a community-focused wellness center that empowers individuals to improve their health routines and live healthier, happier lives."

It's simple, grounded, and full of meaning, a statement she now uses to guide her decisions and stay connected to her purpose.

Here are a few other examples to inspire you:

- Oprah Winfrey: *"To be a teacher and inspire my students to be more than they thought possible."* Vision rooted in growth, impact, and belief in others.

- Simon Sinek: *"To inspire people to do the things that inspire them." A ripple-effect vision that starts with purpose.*

- Melinda Gates: *"A world where every person has the opportunity to live a healthy and productive life."* A clear outcome, deeply human.

- MrBeast: *"To make the world a better place by inspiring others to create lasting change."* A mission powered by creativity and social impact.
- Beyoncé: *"Amplify the beauty in all of us, celebrate empowerment and culture, and drive social change."* A vision grounded in identity, art, and justice.

Each of these tells a story in a sentence, not just what someone wants to *do* but what they want to *change, feel,* or *create.*

When your vision is this clear, goals naturally align. You stop chasing random opportunities and start moving with purpose.

From Vision to Action: Setting Your Goals

A vision without clear goals is just a dream. To make it real, you need specific, measurable steps that build momentum.

Think of your vision like a distant galaxy, full of potential, light, and possibility. But to reach it, you can't just float aimlessly in space. You need to land on solid ground—planet by planet, goal by goal. Each milestone becomes a place to refuel, reflect, and gain momentum for what's next.

That's precisely what Marie did.

After defining her vision, she didn't try to do everything at once. She zoomed in and asked: *What are the most meaningful steps I can take in the next six, twelve, eighteen, and twenty-four months to bring this vision to life?*

She used a few simple principles to shape her goals: clear, time-bound, and written in the present tense to build belief and momentum.

Ooh La La Tip: Setting Goals That Stick

- Be Specific & Time-Bound: Vague goals lead to vague results. Ground your goals in real timelines.
- Prioritize What Matters Most: Focus on three to five goals that directly connect to your vision.
- Use Present Tense: This helps your brain see your goal as something real and achievable.
- Write It Down: You're over 40% more likely to achieve a goal if you write it down.

Marie's Goals: Bringing Her Vision to Life

With her vision as her guide, Marie mapped out four primary goals—each one a stepping stone toward her wellness center dream:

- Within six months: I'm building a strong client base by enrolling at least five loyal clients who trust my expertise and see tangible results in their wellness journey.
- Within twelve months: I'm offering three transformative wellness programs that empower clients to take charge of their health and achieve sustainable lifestyle changes.
- Within eighteen months: I'm leading a high-performing team of three wellness professionals who share my mission of delivering exceptional client experiences.
- Within twenty-four months: I'm running a thriving wellness center that is a trusted hub for community health and well-being.

Each goal brought her closer. With each step, her vision felt less like a dream and more like a destination she was actively building.

Your Turn: Define Your Vision and Goals

Now it's your turn. Let's chart your course toward your *Ooh La La* future, one clear step at a time.

Follow these steps to bring clarity to your destination and set yourself up for success:

1. Envision Your Future – Take time to reflect deeply on the impact you want to make and the life you want to create. Picture it vividly, using the Architect Exercise to bring it to life in your mind.
2. Craft Your Vision Statement – Summarize your future in a powerful, inspiring sentence. Make it clear, concise, and emotionally engaging, like the examples you've seen.
3. Set Your Goals – Define specific, time-bound goals that directly align with your vision. Use the present tense to make them feel real, prioritize what matters most, and write them down to increase your commitment.

Your vision is no longer just a dream; it's become your mission. The clearer it is, the stronger your motivation will be to act. Every decision, every effort, and every step you take from this moment forward should move you closer to your Point B.

With your vision and goals clearly defined, you've set your course. Point B is locked in. You now have a compelling destination that will guide your journey.

But before liftoff, every astronaut must do one critical thing: confirm their launch position.

Mission control pinpoints exactly where the rocket is starting from.

Because without knowing your current coordinates, even the most precise trajectory can miss its mark.

3: POINT A - WHERE ARE YOU TODAY?

Now that your vision is clear, it's time to get grounded.

Before you can move forward, you need to understand exactly where you're starting from. This honest snapshot of your current reality helps you identify the gap between where you are and where you want to be.

Think about your vision:

- Are you building from experience, or starting from scratch?
- Do you have the necessary resources, support, and mindset, or are there areas that require strengthening?

The clearer you are about your present, the more focused and confident you'll be in creating your future.

Mapping Your "O" – Using the *Ooh La La* Scale

Let's take a creative, intuitive look at where you are right now, what we call "O" Mapping.

Picture your life as a circle, an "O." A perfectly round "O" represents balance and fulfillment across all areas of life. However, when one area is neglected or off track, the circle becomes distorted. It becomes uneven, incomplete, and something feels off.

That's where the *Ooh La La* Scale comes in. It helps you evaluate each part of your life on a spectrum:

- *Ooh* – You're struggling, stuck, or dissatisfied.
- *Ooh La* – You're making progress, but there's room to grow.
- *Ooh La La* – You're thriving, aligned, and fulfilled.

This helps you gain clarity, without judgment. Once you spot the imbalances, you can focus on strengthening what needs attention while fully appreciating and nurturing what's already working well.

Key Areas to Map Your "O"

Start by assessing yourself in the following areas on a scale of 1 to 10, with 10 representing an "*Ooh La La*" state: optimal, thriving, and fully aligned with your vision:

1. Career & Business: Are you engaged in work that excites and fulfills you?
2. Financial Independence: Are your finances in a stable and growing position?
3. Health & Fitness: Do you feel strong, energetic, and mentally sharp?
4. Family & Personal Life: Are your relationships supportive and fulfilling?

You can also add areas such as personal growth, community involvement, or spirituality, whatever matters most to you.

Figure 4 – "O" Mapping Concept

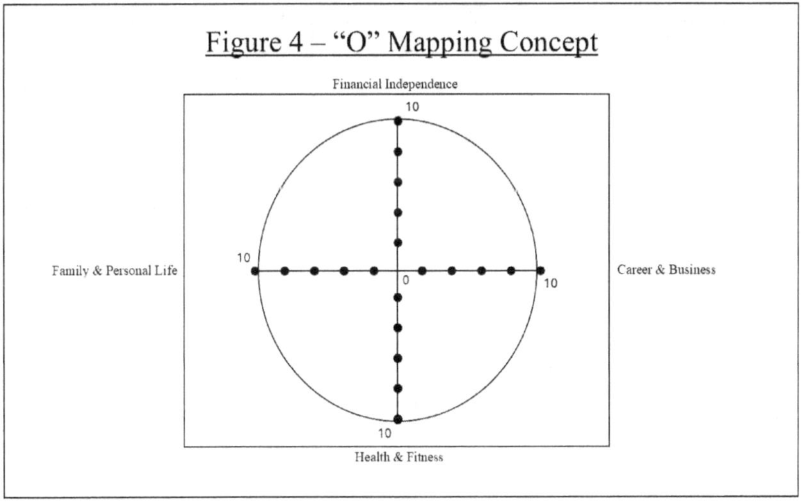

Creating Your O Mapping

1. Rate Yourself: Assign a score from 1-10 for each area based on your current reality.
2. Draw Your O: Imagine plotting each score on a circular diagram. If an area is rated high, it extends outward, creating a fuller shape. Low scores pull parts of the circle inward, forming an uneven or

incomplete "O."

3. Analyze the Shape: Does your circle look whole and balanced? Or does it resemble a misshapen loop with gaps in certain areas?

If your "O" appears full and well-rounded, congratulations—you're operating in *Ooh La La* mode. If it's wobbly or incomplete, some areas need attention before you can truly thrive.

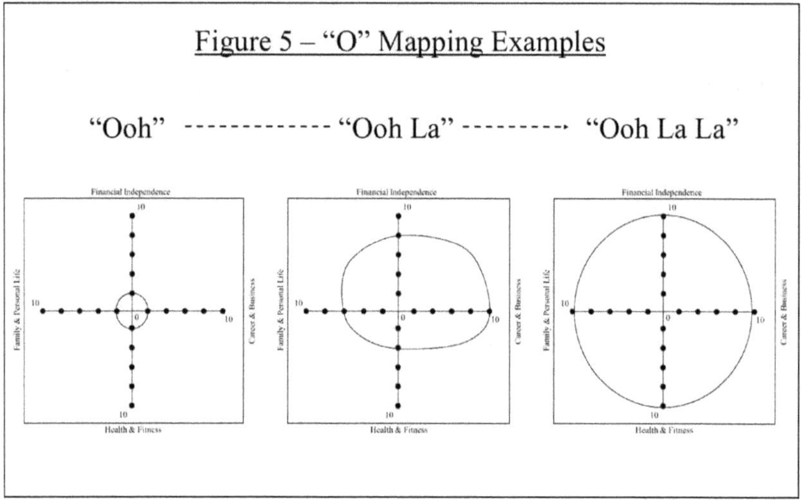

Figure 5 – "O" Mapping Examples

What Your O Reveals

Your O Mapping helps identify which areas need the most focus. If your career and finances are strong, but your health and personal life are struggling, your journey must include strategies to create a more balanced life.

If all areas are in the *Ooh* phase, it's a signal to prioritize foundational growth before taking bold leaps.

This simple yet powerful exercise gives you a visual snapshot of your current standing. It's not about perfection, it's about progress.

As you move through this book, you'll refine your "O" until it becomes a true *Ooh La La*—a life where you're thriving in every area that matters.

So, what does your O look like today?

Permission to Be Honest

Every time I do this exercise, I'm tempted to overrate myself in a few areas, especially the ones I *want* to be thriving in. But the real growth comes from honesty, not perfection.

Creating the "perfect" circle is not the goal here. Some of my most significant breakthroughs started when I admitted, "Okay… this area needs love." That honesty becomes your power.

So, take a breath, get honest with yourself, and remember: wherever you are now is just the starting point. You're not stuck; you're becoming.

Linking Your O Mapping to a Deeper SWOT Analysis

You've probably seen a SWOT analysis before. Maybe a dozen times. Maybe in every corporate workshop, startup course, or team offsite ever. You know the drill: Strengths, Weaknesses, Opportunities, Threats.

But stay with me, because this isn't your typical SWOT.

You've just mapped your "O," so you already know where things feel strong and where they wobble. Now, we're going to dig a little deeper, not in a stiff, spreadsheet way but in a way that actually helps you think more clearly about what's helping or hindering your progress.

So, before your eyes glaze over, let's reintroduce SWOT with a twist.

A Fresh Take on SWOT: The Hare and the Tortoise

Remember the classic fable? The hare races ahead, the tortoise moves slowly but steadily, and somehow, the tortoise wins.

Let's break it down SWOT-style...

The Hare:

- Strengths: Fast, experienced runner, and high confidence.
- Weaknesses: Overconfidence and a tendency to lose focus.
- Opportunities: Clear speed advantage that could secure an easy win.
- Threats: Complacency, underestimating the tortoise, and risk of distraction.

The Tortoise:

- Strengths: Steady pace, strong discipline, and resilience.
- Weaknesses: Slow speed and lack of agility.
- Opportunities: The hare's distractions and overconfidence.
- Threats: Falling too far behind before the hare makes a mistake.

In this fable, the hare ignored his weaknesses and external threats, ultimately leading to his downfall. The tortoise, on the other hand, played to his strengths and used an external opportunity (the hare's distractions) to his advantage.

The lesson? Your success depends not just on your strengths but also on your ability to anticipate and navigate obstacles.

Conducting Your SWOT Analysis

Now it's your turn.

Using the insights from your O Mapping, take a deeper look at what's going on beneath the surface. Let's keep it simple and focused:

- *1. Strengths – What Gives You an Edge?*
  What do you naturally do well? What skills, habits, or experiences can you lean on to make progress?
  Think: talents, support systems, past wins, personal qualities that give you momentum.
- *2. Weaknesses – What Trips You Up?*
  Where do you struggle, hesitate, or feel underprepared?
  Be honest (not harsh)—this is where self-awareness becomes your superpower.
- *3. Opportunities – What's Working in Your Favor?*
  Look around. What resources, trends, or relationships could open doors for you?
  Where do your strengths match up with what's possible right now?
- *4. Threats – What Could Get in the Way?*
  What external factors could slow you down: timing, competition, finances, life responsibilities?
  Knowing these helps you plan smart and stay steady when challenges arise.

Even naming one or two items in each category can reveal powerful insights that help you shape your next move.

Ready? Grab your pen (or digital note) and give your starting point the clarity it deserves.

Figure 6 – SWOT Analysis Template

Strengths	Weaknesses
• ____________ • ____________ • ____________	• ____________ • ____________ • ____________
Opportunities	**Threats**
• ____________ • ____________ • ____________	• ____________ • ____________ • ____________

Applying SWOT in Real Life

To see how this plays out, let's go back to Marie.

After mapping her "O," she realized that while she had deep expertise in wellness and a strong community presence, she lacked experience in business and finance. Her SWOT analysis helped her pinpoint exactly what to focus on next: building financial literacy and leveraging community support to grow her client base.

By clearly identifying her strengths and gaps, Marie could design a smarter, strategic path forward, instead of jumping in blindly.

Bringing It All Together

Your O Mapping gave you a wide-angle view of how aligned your life is across key areas. Your SWOT helped you zoom in, highlighting what's working for you, what's holding you back, and where external forces might help or hinder your growth.

Fundamental transformation begins when you draw a line between where you are and where you want to be. Then, commit to closing that gap.

So, here's a reflection to sit with:

- Are you more like the hare or the tortoise?
- Are you racing ahead, missing blind spots, or moving steadily, building strength with each step?

No matter your pace, your power lies in knowing your tendencies and designing your path with intention.

Awareness gives you data. Now it's time to connect that awareness to something deeper: your reason for moving forward.

That's where your Case for Change comes in.

4: YOUR CASE FOR CHANGE - FROM *"OOH"* TO *"OOH LA LA"*

There comes a moment in every journey when reflection must turn into resolve.

You've seen where you are. You've imagined where you want to be. Now it's time to make the shift from dreaming to deciding.

This is your turning point. The moment you stop treating change like a nice idea, you start treating it as *non-negotiable.*

In the business world, this is called a Case for Change, a clear explanation of why transformation is necessary, what the future could look like, and why it's worth the effort. Companies use it to build alignment and overcome resistance.

But you're not a company. You're a human being. And your change story is personal.

By creating your Case for Change, you'll tap into something deeper than goals: your why. The reason this matters to you. The reason you won't settle for where you've been. The reason you're choosing to grow, even when it's hard.

Let's write the case that makes your transformation real, following a simple yet effective structure:

- Your Destination → Your Vision Statement (where you want to go).
- From → Current State Challenges (where you are now).
- To → Future State Benefits (what transformation looks like).

Think of it as your transformation journey in a single snapshot, a clear path from frustration to fulfillment.

Figure 7 – Case for Change

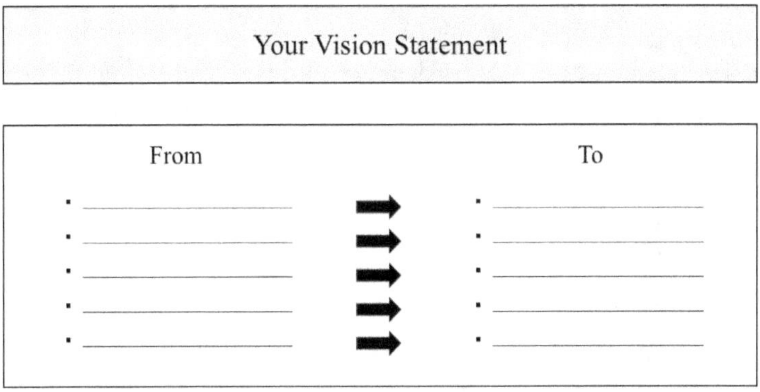

Your Vision Statement

From		To
• ______	➡	• ______
• ______	➡	• ______
• ______	➡	• ______
• ______	➡	• ______
• ______	➡	• ______

Marie's Case for Change: From → To Statements

Let's return to Marie.

After mapping her "O" and digging into her SWOT, Marie saw the truth of where she stood: strong in passion and expertise but facing real gaps in business knowledge, financial independence, and community reach.

She knew she couldn't just hope for change; she had to make it inevitable. So, she wrote her Case for Change, transforming her insights into clear, motivating "From → To" shifts:

Theme	From (*Ooh*: Current Struggles & Limitations)	To (*Ooh La La*: Future Transformation & Benefits)
Empowerment & Ownership	Working for someone else, limited control.	Leading my own wellness center, shaping its mission.
Impact & Community	Passionate about wellness but unable to create lasting impact.	Building a thriving wellness hub that transforms lives.
Business & Financial Growth	Lacking experience, unsure how to scale.	Developing business skills, securing funding, and growing sustainably.

Client Transformation	Helping individuals but unable to offer deep, long-term programs.	Providing personalized wellness programs with lasting results.
Financial Freedom & Fulfillment	Dependent on a 9-to-5 job for security.	Achieving financial independence through meaningful work.

This is Marie's *why*. Her commitment. Her fuel. When things get hard (and they will), she now has a clear reminder of what she's walking away from, and what she's walking toward.

Your Turn: Build Your Case for Change

Now it's your turn to define your transformation.

Using your O Mapping and SWOT insights, write three to five From → To statements that capture the shift you're ready to make.

Ask yourself:

- Where am I feeling stuck or frustrated right now?
- What does "*Ooh La La*" look like in my career, health, finances, or relationships?
- What specific shifts would truly change how I feel and live each day?

These statements make your transformation real: something you can see, feel, and commit to.

Why This Works: The Power of Making It "Stick"

In *Made to Stick*, Chip and Dan Heath explain why some ideas fade while others take hold. The secret? Make them concrete, emotional, and memorable.

A vague goal is easy to postpone. But a clear, emotionally charged transformation becomes part of your identity, something your brain *won't let you ignore.*

Your Case for Change is more than a statement. It's your manifesto—a daily reminder of the life you're building and why it matters.

A Personal Note: My Own "From → To" Transformation

Writing this book has been one of my most meaningful and revealing

Ooh to *Ooh La La* journeys.

Initially, I had ideas and experience but no clear structure. Like many of you, I wrestled with resistance, self-doubt, and the weight of wanting to do something meaningful.

To stay grounded, I created my Case for Change:

Theme	From (*Ooh*: Current Struggles & Limitations)	To (*Ooh La La*: Future Transformation & Benefits)
Clarity & Focus	Having valuable knowledge and stories but no structured way to share them	Creating a clear, actionable framework to help others move from vision to action
Creative Confidence	Questioning whether I had what it takes to write a book that truly helps people	Fully owning my voice and message as a guide for transformation
Impact & Service	Holding onto ideas that could help others but keeping them inside	Sharing tools that empower others to lead, grow, and create meaningful change
Personal Growth & Mastery	Letting doubt and distraction delay progress	Committing fully to the process—learning, growing, and showing up even when it's hard

These shifts became my compass. They reminded me that this journey was not just about finishing a book; it was about helping you launch your next chapter.

By now, you have mapped your "O," explored your strengths and gaps, and built a solid Case for Change that makes quitting no longer an option.

Before we move into action planning, the "how," there is one more piece that will shape your success, a key component of awareness: your mindset.

No strategy or roadmap can match the power of a strong and resilient mindset. In the next chapter, we will explore the mental shifts that will help you sustain momentum, overcome challenges, and step fully into your *Ooh La La* life.

Your transformation has already begun. Now, let us make sure you have the mindset to carry it all the way.

OOH LA LA HIGHLIGHTS

STEP 3: DEFINE A CLEAR VISION

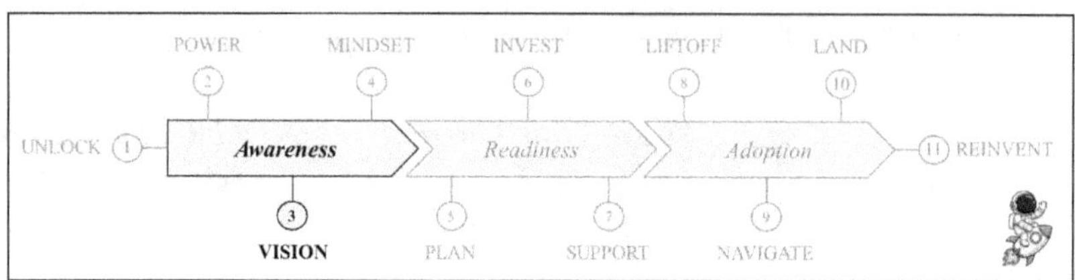

MISSION BRIEF

Defining a bold future starts with clarity—knowing where you are now (Point A), where you're going (Point B), and what's driving you forward (your Case for Change). When these elements align, your goals shift from nice-to-have ideas into must-do missions.

CRITICAL SYSTEMS ANALYSIS

- The ABC Model structures your journey:
    - Point A – Your current state: an honest look at where you are right now.
    - Point B – Your vision: a vivid picture of the life you want to create.
    - Point C – The constraints and obstacles that may arise (coming in Part II).
    - *Ooh La La Tip:* Start with Point B to let yourself dream big without the limitations of your current reality.
- Point B: Your vision anchors you.
    - It provides direction, motivation, and focus.
    - A vivid, well-defined vision becomes your internal compass: guiding decisions, fueling resilience, and helping you stay on course.
    - Craft a personal vision statement to guide your direction and inspire consistent action.
    - Translate that vision into three to five specific, time-bound goals that turn intention into momentum.

- Point A: Know your starting point.
    - O Mapping gives you a visual of how balanced your life is across key areas.
        - A complete "O" = thriving. A wobbly one = some areas need attention.
    - SWOT Analysis helps you dig deeper:
        - *Strengths*: What you can lean on.
        - *Weaknesses*: What may slow you down.
        - *Opportunities*: What could accelerate your growth.
        - *Threats*: What risks you need to watch for.
    - Together, O Mapping and SWOT provide a clear and honest snapshot of where you're truly starting from.
- Your Case for Change transforms insight into action.
    - It turns your vision into a mission by defining what's at stake.
    - Your Case for Change includes:
        - A powerful vision statement.
        - Clear From → To shifts that capture the transformation you're committing to.
    - When your reason for change is real and personal, following through becomes non-negotiable.

PILOT'S REFLECTION

1. Is your vision clear, specific, and motivating?
2. What did your O Mapping and SWOT reveal about your strengths and gaps?
3. Have you written a Case for Change that genuinely matters to you, and reminds you why you won't give up?

NEXT COORDINATES

With your destination now set, it's time to fuel the mindset that will take you there. In the next chapter, we'll explore the mental shifts required to stay the course when the road ahead gets tough.

CHAPTER 4

•

CULTIVATE A WINNER'S MINDSET

1: DEVELOPING AN *"OOH LA LA"* MINDSET

Picture this: you're two weeks into pursuing your bold new goal. You started strong; vision mapped, goals clarified, action underway. But then… life happens. A setback. An unexpected delay. A wave of doubt that whispers, *"Maybe I'm not cut out for this."*

Sound familiar?

You're not alone. This is the make-or-break moment every dreamer faces when the initial excitement fades and the first real turbulence hits. It's not your ability or your plan that determines what happens next; it's your mindset.

Your mindset is the operating system behind your entire mission. If it's outdated, buggy, or full of limiting beliefs, even the most brilliant strategy will eventually stall. Like a rocket with the wrong trajectory, you'll burn all your fuel without reaching orbit.

That's why now, more than ever, it's time to upgrade.

And just like our *Ooh La La* Scale for success, your mindset exists on a spectrum:

Ooh → Stuck in fear and self-doubt, convinced that abilities are fixed.

Ooh La → Open to growth but still hesitant when setbacks arise.

Ooh La La → Fully embracing challenges, learning from failure, and striving for continuous improvement.

This chapter is about helping you shift, step by step, into *Ooh La La* mode, where your mindset becomes your launch fuel, not your handbrake.

Let's dive into what that looks like and how to get there.

The *"Ooh La La"* Growth Mindset Assessment

An *Ooh La La* mindset is rooted in growth; the belief that skills, intelligence, and success are built through effort, curiosity, and learning. Unlike a fixed mindset, where you believe that you're either "good at something" or "not," a growth mindset thrives on the idea that everything is a skill that can be improved.

So how do you know where you stand?

Let's put your mindset through the *Ooh La La* test.

Ooh: Stuck in a Fixed Mindset

- Challenges are threats. Avoids anything that might expose weaknesses.
- Failure is final. Believes that mistakes define ability.
- Effort feels pointless. Thinks, "If I were talented, this would be easy."
- Criticism is personal. Feels attacked when receiving feedback.
- Others' success is threatening. Thinks, "They're just lucky" or "I'll never be that good."

Ooh La: Testing the Growth Mindset

- Challenges are uncomfortable but worth it.
- Failure is hard, but lessons are starting to make sense.
- Effort feels valuable, but doubt still creeps in.
- Criticism is accepted but sometimes stings.
- Others' success is inspiring, but comparison is still a struggle.

Ooh La La: A Fully Growth-Oriented Mindset

- Challenges are exciting! They lead to breakthroughs.
- Failure is feedback; each mistake is a stepping stone to mastery.
- Effort is the price of success. Hard work pays off, no exceptions.
- Criticism is welcome. Learning from others makes you better.

- Others' success is proof of what's possible. It's motivation, not a threat.

So, where do you land? *Ooh*? *Ooh La*? Or are you living in *Ooh La La* mode?

The good news is that no matter where you start, your mindset is malleable. One of the clearest ways to determine where you stand on the mindset spectrum is how you respond to adversity.

This brings us to a practical extension of the growth mindset: how you show up in challenging moments, what we call the Victor vs. Victim response.

Are You Responding Like a Victor or a Victim?

When life gets bumpy, and it will, your mindset either propels you forward or pulls you down. That moment of pressure is when you reveal what kind of mindset you're truly operating with.

Think of it like this:

A growth mindset is what you believe about your potential. A Victor or Victim response is how you behave when that belief gets tested.

To help visualize this, imagine an invisible accountability line running through every challenge you face.

- When you operate above the line, you're in Victor mode: taking responsibility, staying empowered, learning from feedback, and looking for solutions.
- When you slip below the line, you're in Victim mode: blaming others, avoiding accountability, or feeling powerless in the face of setbacks.

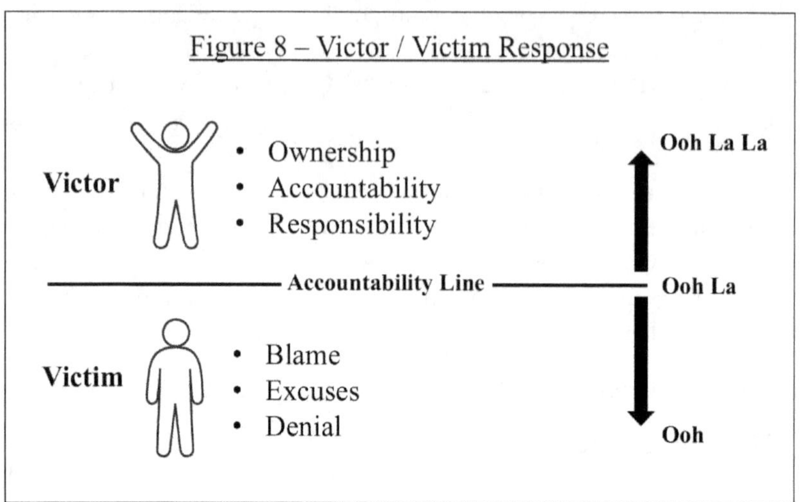

What matters most in this moment is awareness, not judgment. Everyone dips below the line from time to time. The goal is to notice it, then climb back up. That's how you build mental resilience.

Mindset Response	**Below the Line (Victim – *Ooh*)**	**Transitional (*Ooh La*)**	**Above the Line (Victor – *Ooh La La!*)**
Challenges	"Why is this happening to me?"	"This is tough, but I'll try."	"Bring it on—I grow through challenges!"
Failure	"I knew I wasn't good enough."	"That was rough… I'll try a different approach."	"That was a valuable lesson—I'm stronger now!"
Effort	"It shouldn't be this hard."	"I'll keep trying, but I doubt it'll work."	"Hard work pays off. Let's do this!"
Feedback	"They're just being critical."	"Maybe there's something useful in this."	"Great! Now I know how to improve!"
Others' Success	"It's not fair they're ahead of me."	"I'm happy for them… but when will it be my turn?"	"Their success proves what's possible—I'm next!"

When you can consistently shift your reactions from below the line to above it, you're not just thinking with a growth mindset, you're living it. This is what the *Ooh La La* mindset looks like in action.

How to Stay in *"Ooh La La"* Mode

Building a growth mindset is like training a muscle; it's not a one-time flex but a daily workout. The goal isn't to be perfect but to develop habits that reinforce your *Ooh La La* mindset over time.

Here's how:

1. Challenge Yourself to Level Up
    - Instead of avoiding difficulty, seek out challenges that force you to grow. Just like a rocket needs a massive force to break Earth's gravity, you need challenges to break old patterns and launch forward.
    - *Ooh La La Tip: Ask yourself, "What challenge can I take on this week that will make me stronger?"*
2. Embrace the "Fail Forward" Mindset
    - If you're not failing, you're not growing. Every expert was once a beginner who made thousands of mistakes. The difference? They didn't quit.
    - *Ooh La La Tip: Reframe failure as a tuition fee for success. Every mistake you make is an investment in your growth.*
3. Surround Yourself with "*Ooh La La*" People
    - Mindsets are contagious. If you surround yourself with *Ooh*-minded people who complain, blame, and stay stuck, you'll likely adopt the same habits. Instead, seek out people who challenge, inspire, and uplift you.
    - *Ooh La La Tip: Find a mentor, accountability partner, or mastermind group that operates in Ooh La La mode.*
4. Master the Power of Self-Talk
    - Your inner dialogue shapes your reality. If you constantly tell yourself, "I'm not good at this," your brain will find ways to make that statement true. Flip the script!
    - *Ooh La La Tip: Replace limiting beliefs with affirmations like "I am capable of learning anything with effort and time."*

5. Track Your Progress & Celebrate Wins
    - Progress fuels motivation. Instead of obsessing over how far you have left to go, celebrate how far you've already come.
    - *Ooh La La Tip: Keep an Ooh La La journal where you note:*
        - *Challenges you tackled.*
        - *Failures you learned from.*
        - *Small wins that brought you closer to your goal.*

Final Thought: The Mindset of a Winner

At its core, an *Ooh La La* mindset is the belief that growth is always possible, failure is just feedback, and you are capable of far more than you know.

So, are you ready to upgrade your inner operating system and show up as the winner you truly are?

Your mission: To leave the "*Ooh*" behind, embrace the growth from the transitional "*Ooh La*," and step fully into the confident, thriving "*Ooh La La*" version of yourself.

Are you ready to make the shift?

2: YOU BECOME WHAT YOU THINK ABOUT

A few years ago, I planted a garden with my daughter. We chose each seed carefully, feeling the cool soil slip through our fingers as we pictured the blooms they would one day become. Day after day, we tended the earth until the first shoots appeared. In that quiet growth, I saw the truth: just as a garden springs from the seeds we plant, our lives grow from the thoughts we choose to nurture.

Each day, your mind sows ideas; some drift away, while others take root, shaping your choices, your actions, and the course of your life. Those thoughts are your internal navigation system, quietly charting the path ahead.

Your Mind: The Flight Computer of Your Mission

In space travel, the onboard flight computer is one of the most critical components of the mission. It processes millions of calculations per second, adjusting the spacecraft's trajectory, fine-tuning its course, and ensuring it stays locked onto its destination.

But here's the catch: the computer doesn't decide the destination, the astronaut does.

Your mind works the same way. It will process and amplify whatever you feed it.

- If you program it with self-doubt, fear, and negativity, your system fills with error codes, is constantly recalibrating, and is unsure of where to go.
- If you input confidence, focus, and positive expectations, your system locks in on success, filtering distractions and keeping you aligned with your mission.

This aligns with the *Ooh La La* Scale:

- *Ooh* (Unfocused Mind): Your system is filled with conflicting instructions. The spacecraft drifts, unsure where to go.
- *Ooh La* (Adjusting Focus): You begin fine-tuning your thoughts, adjusting your mental programming, but occasional errors still require correction.
- *Ooh La La* (Fully Locked In): The flight computer is set, the course is locked, and your mind navigates toward success with laser precision.

Have you ever decided on a car you want to buy, only to suddenly see it everywhere? It's not that more of those cars appeared overnight; your brain simply tuned in to noticing them. This is known as selective attention, and it works similarly to achieve goals.

Think of your brain as the astronaut's targeting system. Once you set a goal, your mind begins to filter out distractions and focus on opportunities that align with your mission.

- Want to start a business? You'll begin noticing conversations, books, and resources that can help.
- Focused on improving your health? Suddenly, you'll hear about fitness programs and meet like-minded people.

Your mind didn't create these opportunities; it simply became aware of them because you set your mental GPS.

Your thoughts program your internal navigation system, deciding your trajectory. If you aren't happy with your current results, it's time to ask:

What thoughts am I planting? Is my flight computer locked onto my dream destination, or am I drifting aimlessly through space?

The Thoughts / Outcomes Connection

Understanding this connection is key to mastering your mindset. Imagine climbing a mountain.

Figure 9 – Thoughts / Outcomes Connection

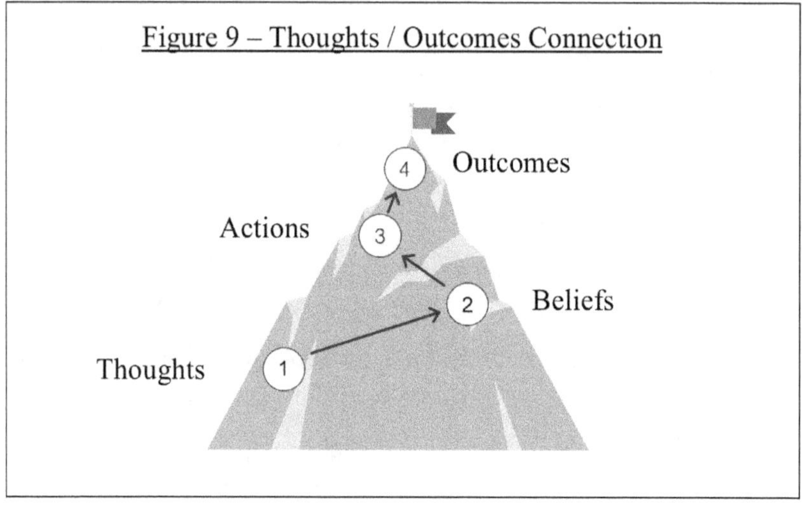

Each step builds on the one before:

1. Thoughts (Bottom of the Mountain): The seeds you plant. If you plant negative thoughts, you grow obstacles. If you plant positive ones, you build momentum.

2. Beliefs (Higher on the Mountain): Your repeated thoughts shape your beliefs. If you keep thinking, "I'm not good enough," it becomes a belief that limits your potential.

3. Actions (Even Higher on the Mountain): Your beliefs dictate how you act. If you believe in your ability to succeed, you take decisive, confident steps. If not, you hesitate and hold back.

4. Outcomes (Top of the Mountain): Your actions determine your reality. If your thoughts and beliefs were strong, you would achieve *Ooh La La* success. If they were filled with doubt, you remain stuck at *Ooh*.

How to Reprogram Your Mental Navigation System

The good news? You're the astronaut, so you can reprogram your flight computer anytime.

Many of the strategies you've already explored in the Growth Mindset section apply here, reinforcing the importance of staying "above the line" and embracing a Victor mentality.

Here's how to keep your mind locked onto success:

- Challenge & Reframe Negative Thoughts: When a self-defeating thought appears, ask: Is this helping or hindering my mission? If it's holding you back, reframe it: "I'm still learning, and every step moves me forward."
- Stay Above the Line: Lead your mind toward action and solutions, not blame or stagnation.
- Focus on What You Want: Program your mental GPS with clear, positive destinations so your brain seeks paths to make them real.
- Visualize Success: Like astronauts, mentally rehearse achieving your goal every day.
- Practice Gratitude: Identify three things you're grateful for daily to shift your mindset toward abundance and optimism.

Locking in Your Mindset - System Check

Your mind is constantly transmitting signals, whether you're aware of it or not. By now, you've learned how thoughts shape belief, how belief drives action, and how action creates outcomes.

So, let's run a systems check:

- Are your daily thoughts aligned with your destination or your distractions?
- Are your beliefs empowering or limiting your ascent?
- Are your actions coming from fear or from purpose?

Now, revisit the *Ooh La La* spectrum for your mindset one last time but through this upgraded lens:

Mindset Mode	Thought Pattern	Belief	Action	Outcome
Ooh	"This won't work."	I'm not good enough.	Avoid or delay.	Stay stuck.

Ooh La	"Maybe I can."	I'm learning.	Small, tentative steps.	Mixed results.
Ooh La La	"This is mine to build."	I grow through action.	Bold, focused moves.	Momentum and traction.

If you're not loving your current trajectory, don't abandon the mission; adjust the course.

Your mind is your most powerful flight system; tune it to your highest potential, and the mission becomes inevitable.

3: GOT FEARS?

Let's be real, fear shows up the moment you decide to do something big. It sneaks in before the big presentation, lurks behind bold business ideas, and whispers doubts when you're on the edge of a life-changing decision. That pit in your stomach? That's fear whispering, "What if you fail? What if you're not good enough?"

What if fear wasn't a roadblock but a sign you're on the verge of something extraordinary? What if fear wasn't there to stop you but to tell you: "This is worth it."

It's time to stop seeing fear as an enemy and start using it as fuel because every great mission begins with stepping into the unknown.

What's Behind the Big Black Door?

There's an old fable about a criminal facing execution. He could choose: a noose, or a large, dark, iron Black Door. The criminal hesitated, glancing at the imposing door, its sheer presence filling him with dread. After a moment, he chose the rope.

As the noose tightened around his neck, he turned to the king and asked, "What's behind the door?"

The king chuckled. "You know, it's funny, I offer everyone the same choice, and nearly all of them choose the rope."

"But why? What's behind the door?" the man pressed, now desperate to know.

The king's smile faded as he answered simply: "Freedom. But people are so afraid of the unknown that they prefer the certainty of their limitations."

This story serves as a powerful reminder of how fear can hold us back. The criminal was allowed to step into something new, yet his fear of the unknown made him choose the only fate he could see, one that guaranteed his end.

How often do we do the same? How many times have we opted for the familiar, even when it meant staying stuck, instead of pushing open the door to something greater?

Marie had a "Black Door" moment, too.

For years, she thrived in a stable, respected corporate role. Yet beneath the predictability, an entrepreneurial spark kept calling. When the chance came to open her own wellness center, fear surged; what if she failed, went unnoticed, or lost her credibility?

Her Black Door wasn't made of wood or steel; it was a choice: remain in a system that no longer fueled her growth or step into the unknown to build something that truly reflected her purpose.

Marie chose the door.

It wasn't easy. But it was transformational.

And she's not alone:

- A stage actor faced her Black Door moment when she decided to stop auditioning for roles that drained her and instead create her one-woman show—something raw, real, and hers.
- A passionate home cook took the leap to turn her side hustle into a full-fledged catering business, trading perfection for progress, and finally sharing her flavors with the world.
- And a quiet illustrator decided to publish his first digital comic series, moving past fear and into visibility, ready to turn his art into something public and impactful.

The Black Door shows up differently for all of us.

But it always demands courage.

So, ask yourself: What's my big Black Door? The business idea you've been sitting on? The leap you've hesitated to take? The creative project that won't leave you alone? The *Ooh La La* version of yourself waiting on the other side?

Every significant opportunity comes wrapped in uncertainty, but just beyond it could be your path to *Ooh La La*, waiting for you to step through.

Fear will always be there. The question is, will you let it keep you from what's on the other side?

You have two choices: Stay where you are or walk through the door.

Fear: The Signal That You're on the Right Path

Here is what I have found: Fear only shows up when you're standing at the edge of something that matters. Fear is not here to stop you but to signal that you're moving beyond your comfort zone, into real growth.

Think about it: If your dreams didn't scare you, would they even be worth pursuing?

- Fear and the Comfort Zone
  Your comfort zone is like Earth's atmosphere; it feels safe, predictable, and familiar. But nothing groundbreaking happens inside it. Astronauts don't experience the vastness of space by staying on the launchpad. The magic happens when they push past gravity and step into the unknown.

- Fear as Self-Discovery
  Facing fear forces you to confront what you're capable of. It stretches you, challenges you, and ultimately proves that you are stronger than you think. Fear reveals your hidden strengths, and once you see them, you can't unsee them.

- Fear as a Growth Indicator
  Fear is your body's way of saying, "Hey, we're about to do something new here!" Instead of letting it hold you back, start recognizing it as a signal that you're on the edge of a breakthrough.

Turning Fear into Rocket Fuel

Fear won't disappear, but you can learn to use it to fuel your momentum. Here's how:

1. Reframe Fear as Excitement
   Fear and excitement feel the same physically: racing heart, sweaty palms, adrenaline rush. The difference? How you interpret it. Instead of saying, "I'm terrified," try saying, "I'm excited for this challenge." The moment you shift your perspective, fear loses its grip.

2. Take the First Step (No Matter How Small)
   Fear thrives on inaction. The longer you wait, the bigger it gets. The best way to shrink fear? Move. Even the smallest step, such as making

a call, writing a plan, or speaking up in a meeting, turns fear into momentum.

3. Play the "What's the Worst That Could Happen?" Game
   Ask yourself: What's the worst thing that could happen if I try? Most of the time, the worst-case scenario isn't nearly as bad as we imagine. And even if things don't go as planned, you'll learn, adapt, and come back stronger.

4. Visualize Your *Ooh La La* Self
   Picture yourself after you've faced your fear. How does it feel? What did you gain? Visualization helps you step into that future version of yourself and reminds you why pushing past fear is worth it.

5. Surround Yourself with People Who Push You Forward
   Even astronauts have a ground crew. The people you surround yourself with can either amplify your fears or help you rise above them. Choose mentors, friends, and supporters who challenge you, encourage you, and remind you of what's possible.

My Fear: Writing This Book

I have to say, writing this book terrified me.

What if no one reads it? What if critics hate it? What if it's not *Ooh La La* enough?

The doubts were loud. I worried about what my colleagues would think, what my family would say, and whether I even had the right to write a book on success. After all, I had only co-written a police novel with my dad (in French, no less!). Writing a business book? That felt like stepping into deep space without a safety harness.

But then I thought about you, the person reading this, looking for clarity, motivation, and a roadmap to your dreams. If this book helps even one person push past their fears and act, then overcoming my own fears was worth it.

So, I did what I'm asking you to do. I walked through the big Black Door. I hit "publish." I stepped into the unknown.

Now, I'm asking you to do the same. Fear is your co-pilot, strapped in beside you, whispering, "You're about to do something incredible."

So what will you do? Stay grounded in "*Ooh*," staring at the Black Door, and wondering "what if"? Or take the controls, push the throttle, and launch straight into your *Ooh La La*?

The choice is yours. Strap in and go!

4. YOU ARE ALREADY SUCCESSFUL

As we close this chapter on cultivating the mindset of a winner, it's time to recognize something important: you're already successful.

Wait, what?

You might be thinking, "But I haven't even achieved my big goal yet!"

That's okay. Success begins the moment you find the courage to step onto the track, long before the finish line.

Earl Nightingale, a pioneer in personal development, defined success clearly and powerfully as *"The progressive realization of a worthy ideal."*

In other words, you're successful the moment you begin pursuing a meaningful goal, one that you've chosen intentionally, not one handed to you by someone else.

The real win? Refusing to live life on autopilot. Choosing direction over drift. Designing your life instead of defaulting to someone else's blueprint.

By defining your vision, embracing change, and strengthening your mindset, you've done what many never will; you've taken control of your path.

Success is less about the outcome and more about the commitment. It's about waking up with intention, taking action aligned with your purpose, and continuing forward even when it's hard. That's what separates growth from stagnation.

Like an astronaut preparing for launch, success starts with the decision to rise, the preparation behind the scenes, and the steady pursuit of a mission that matters.

You're not waiting for success to happen someday.
You're living it, right now.

Marie's Success—Long Before the Destination

Let's revisit Marie, our inspiring wellness entrepreneur. Has she built her wellness center yet? Not quite. However, she has a vision: *To create a community-focused wellness center that empowers individuals to enhance their health routines and lead healthier, happier lives.*

She has mapped out her plan, taken her first steps, and is fully committed to making it happen. And that's why she's already successful. Her success isn't defined by a grand opening ribbon-cutting ceremony. It's in every intentional step she takes to make her dream a reality.

Her journey reminds us once again that success is based on the clarity of your why and the consistency of your actions.

You Have a Vision—You Are Already Successful

By now, you've defined your vision. You know what you want. That alone sets you apart from many people who drift through life without a clear direction.

Does that mean you have all the answers yet? Of course not, and you don't need to.

So, take a moment to appreciate just how far you've already come.

You've started. You've shown up. You're serious about your goals and that's worth celebrating.

Now that you've locked in your destination, it's time for the next part—Readiness.

If Part 1 was about defining the mission, Part 2 is about preparing for launch.

Astronauts don't strap into a rocket without meticulous planning, and you shouldn't launch your mission without it either. Your goals deserve strategy, investment, and a support system to help you navigate the journey ahead.

In Part 2, we'll focus on:

- Developing Your Launch Plan – Turning your vision and goals into an actionable, step-by-step plan.
- Investing in Yourself – Building the skills and habits you need to thrive.
- Assembling Your Crew – Creating the support system that will help you stay on course.

Success is a team sport, and the more prepared you are, the smoother your takeoff will be.

So, buckle up because in the next phase, we're getting ready to launch. And trust me, it's going to be *Ooh La La.*

OOH *LA LA* HIGHLIGHTS

STEP 4: CULTIVATE A WINNER'S MINDSET

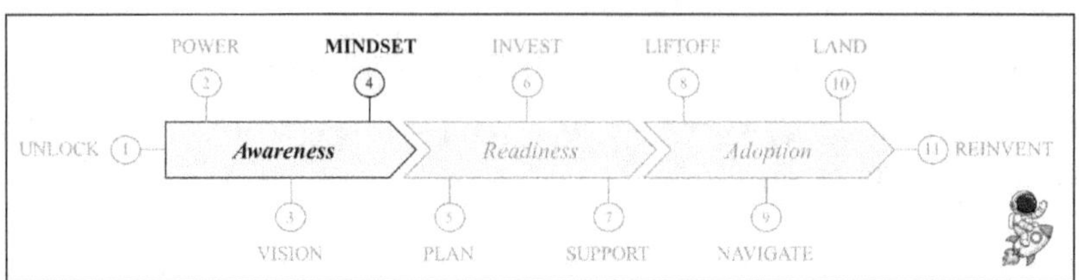

MISSION BRIEF

A strong mindset is a key to sustaining momentum and overcoming challenges on your journey. Just like an operating system determines how everything else functions, your mindset influences how you process challenges, pursue goals, and respond under pressure. Developing an *Ooh La La* mindset means shifting from hesitation and fear to confidence and resilience—allowing you to embrace growth and transformation fully.

CRITICAL SYSTEMS ANALYSIS

- Mindset operates on a spectrum:
  - *Ooh* – Stuck in self-doubt and fear, avoiding challenges.
  - *Ooh La* – Open to growth but still hesitant when facing setbacks.
  - *Ooh La La* – Fully committed to learning, growing, and pushing past limits.
- Victim vs. Victor Response:
  - Victims feel powerless, blame circumstances, and avoid responsibility.
  - Victors take ownership, embrace challenges, and use setbacks as stepping stones.
- Your mind is like an astronaut's flight computer; whatever you program into it determines your trajectory.
  - Negative thoughts can create mental drift, leading to feelings of uncertainty.
  - A focused, growth-oriented mindset locks in your course toward

success.

- Fear is a natural part of the growth process. Instead of seeing fear as a roadblock, recognize it as a signal that you're stepping into something meaningful.
- Success is about committing to the journey. Every step taken toward your vision means you're already successful.

PILOT'S REFLECTION

1. Where does your mindset currently fall on the *Ooh La La* Scale? What update or reboot is needed?
2. How do you respond to challenges? Are you operating in a Victor or Victim mode?
3. What limiting beliefs are running in the background and how can you reprogram them into empowering thoughts?

NEXT COORDINATES

Your mindset is now mission-ready. In Part II, we shift from inner work to external preparation, translating vision into a strategic and actionable plan to endure liftoff and beyond.

PART II

•

Readiness

Preparing for Liftoff

CHAPTER 5

•

YOUR LAUNCH PLAN

1. CRAFTING YOUR MISSION BLUEPRINT

You've dreamt big. You've cleared the mental fog. You've mapped your mission. Now comes the thrilling part: execution—turning all that clarity into real-world magic.

You have probably heard the saying: *"A dream without a plan is just a wish."* Enthusiasm alone won't get you to your destination. If astronauts just "winged it" after takeoff, their mission would fail. Every great achievement, whether launching a rocket, building a creative venture, or transforming your life, requires a structured plan to turn bold ideas into real success.

But wait… strategic planning? That sounds complicated. Do you need it?

Absolutely—but we're keeping it simple. Let's not drown in spreadsheets or hire consultants to map out your next move. Instead, you need a clear, actionable Mission Blueprint; a structured plan that bridges the gap between where you are now and where you want to be.

To achieve this, we'll walk through powerful tools that help you take bold ideas and turn them into smart plans. Each of these tools—OKRs, the X Factor, and the TOWS Matrix—acts as a booster, providing structure, focus, and adaptability.

You don't need to master them all at once. Think of this chapter as a toolkit, not a checklist. Take what resonates most right now and trust that you can return to the rest as your mission evolves.

Let's build your plan!

Why a Mission Blueprint Matters

Imagine planning a cross-country road trip. You know your destination, but without a map or key checkpoints, you risk getting lost, running out of fuel, or taking unnecessary detours.

Your Mission Blueprint serves the same purpose for your goals:

- It keeps you on course so you don't waste time on distractions.
- It ensures steady progress with clear milestones.
- It helps you navigate challenges instead of getting stuck.

To keep things simple and actionable, we'll use a powerful yet easy-to-use tool to structure your plan: OKRs—short for Objectives and Key Results.

OKRs: Your Personal Mission Control

OKRs, trusted by top companies like Google and Apple, aren't just for businesses. They are powerful tools for any meaningful goal, helping you stay focused, measure progress, and hold yourself accountable.

Think of OKRs like building a bridge across a canyon:

- Your Objective is the far side, the destination.
- Your Key Results are the checkpoints showing you're getting closer.
- Your Key Activities are the planks you lay down to move forward, one step at a time.

Here's how to use them:

1. Objective (O) – Where do you want to go?
   This is your short-to-mid-term goal, the one that brings your bigger Vision to life.
   You already defined these goals in Chapter 3 when you mapped out your mission.
2. Key Results (KR) – How will you measure progress?
   These are clear, measurable milestones that show you're on the right path.

3. Key Activities – What actions will get you there?
   The consistent, focused tasks that generate real momentum.

Think of it like this:

- Your Vision → The inspiring big picture (your Point B)
- Your Goals/Objectives → What success looks like on the path toward that vision
- Key Results → How you'll measure real progress
- Key Activities → The practical steps that make it happen

Meet Alex: Launching a Financial YouTube Channel

In Part I, we followed Marie's journey as she uncovered the heart of her vision. Now, let's introduce Alex.

Like Marie, he found himself at a turning point. Alex is a financial advisor with over a decade of experience helping clients grow their wealth. His world revolves around spreadsheets, strategies, and long-term plans. But recently something shifted. He felt a pull toward something bigger: teaching everyday people to take control of their finances at scale, not just one-on-one.

That vision—the big one—is to become a trusted voice in financial education, reaching people worldwide through digital platforms.

To bring that long-term dream closer to reality, Alex identified one clear, tangible goal to focus on first: *Grow a financial YouTube channel to 10,000 subscribers within one year.*

Initially, the idea seemed overwhelming. He wasn't sure where to begin, how to stand out, or whether anyone would even tune in. But he also knew that vague ambition wouldn't get him there. He needed structure. A roadmap. Something to keep him accountable.

That's where his Mission Blueprint came in.

Alex's Mission Blueprint Using OKRs

Alex began by creating a simple OKR—Objectives and Key Results—plan to move his idea from concept to execution.

Objective:

Launch a successful financial YouTube channel and reach 10,000 subscribers within one year.

Key Results:

- By Month Three: Publish twenty-four high-quality videos and gain 1,000 subscribers.
- By Month Six: Reach 5,000 subscribers and maintain an average of 500 views per video.
- By Month Nine: Collaborate with at least three other financial influencers to expand his reach.
- By Month Twelve: Reach 10,000 subscribers and average 1,000 views per video.

Each Key Result gave him a measurable milestone. It was a trackable plan with built-in accountability.

Laying the Bridge: Alex's Key Activities

With his milestones defined, Alex got practical. He didn't need to master everything overnight; he just needed to take the right actions consistently.

To reach his Month Three target—*twenty-four videos and 1,000 subscribers*—he focused on five priority activities:

- Plan & Script Video Content
  Research trending financial topics, outline clear and actionable scripts, and speak with empathy, not jargon.

- Film & Edit with Consistency
  Establish a home setup with decent lighting and sound. Record weekly. Edit for clarity and energy.

- Optimize for Search & Clicks
  Use strong titles, thumbnail images, and keyword-rich descriptions to improve discoverability.

- Share Across Platforms
  Post videos on LinkedIn, X, and relevant financial forums to expand reach beyond YouTube's algorithm.

- Track Performance & Adjust
  Use analytics to see what's working, then tweak future content accordingly.

This was his launchpad. Not a scattered to-do list but a focused plan tied directly to a measurable goal. Every action served a purpose: to build trust, grow reach, and move steadily toward that 10,000-subscriber milestone.

My Own Mission Blueprint: Writing This Book

Just like Alex, I wasn't immune to uncertainty.

My vision was clear, but vision alone doesn't finish a book. I needed the same structure, clarity, and accountability. So, I created my own Mission Blueprint.

Without a plan, I knew I would get lost in distractions and, even worse, let doubts derail me. It would have been easy to stay stuck in research, procrastinate on design, or endlessly rethink my direction. So, I got specific. I gave my goal a clear name and set a timeline.

Objective:
Write and publish Be *Ooh La La* by December 2025.

Key Results:

- Create a detailed outline by November 2024
- Write the first draft of Part I by January 2025
- Write the first draft of Part II by March 2025
- Write the first draft of Part III by May 2025
- Edit, proofread, and format the layout by August 2025
- Conduct pre-launch activities by October 2025
- Publish by December 2025

By breaking it down this way, the goal became less overwhelming and more actionable. Instead of saying "I want to write a book," I had a structure, with real milestones and momentum.

It didn't make the process effortless, but it made it possible. And that's the power of a plan.

Refining & Elevating Your Plan: The Power of Iteration

You've mapped out your goal, defined your Key Results, and outlined the specific activities that will move you forward. Now, take a step back and assess your Mission Blueprint.

Where does it stand on the *Ooh La La* Scale?

- Is it still in the "*Ooh*" phase—unclear, scattered, missing key details?
- Is it "*Ooh La*"—starting to take shape but could use some fine-tuning?

- Or is it "*Ooh La La*"—structured, motivating, and ready for action?
- If you're somewhere between *Ooh* and *Ooh La*, don't worry! A great plan isn't built in one sitting.

Here's the secret: The best planners are not only disciplined but adaptable. Give yourself space to refine it. Some of your best insights will come in unexpected moments: while showering, driving, or daydreaming.

Your plan should guide you, not trap you. Flexibility is key. Make sure it excites you. If your blueprint doesn't spark motivation, tweak it until it does. Give yourself permission to adjust; every iteration brings you closer to success.

So, step away for a moment. Let your mind wander. Then come back, fine-tune your blueprint, and get moving.

Your plan is coming together. Now, it's time to ruthlessly prioritize, not by doing more but by locking in on the one action that moves everything forward.

Let's sharpen your focus and take your execution to the next level. Onward!

2. THE X FACTOR

You've built a blueprint. Now it's time to power it up with precision.

Having a plan is a strong start, but execution is where the real transformation happens. However, not all actions are created equal. Some will launch you forward like a rocket; others will keep you spinning in place. If you want to reach *Ooh La La*—the place where growth feels aligned, electric, and inevitable—you need to focus on what moves the needle most.

This is where your X Factor comes in: It is the one activity that, if prioritized above all else, will create the greatest impact on your goal.

What is Your X Factor?

Imagine this: a bustling international airport, humming with the energy of thousands of travelers, but behind the scenes, chaos was unfolding. Bags were vanishing from conveyors, passengers' frustration was boiling over, flights were delayed one after another, and customer service lines stretched endlessly as overwhelmed agents struggled to keep up. The baggage team had tried everything, rebooting systems, calling in extra hands, and manually rerouting luggage, but the delays only deepened like a snowball rolling downhill.

After two relentless days, the airport's leadership brought in a specialist, an expert in untangling complex transportation snafus. She arrived with calm focus, stepping into the nerve center of operations. Her eyes scanned the control room, then trailed along the serpentine conveyor belts. She sifted through scan logs, tracing each piece of luggage like a detective following clues.

Then, tucked away in a quiet corner of the sorting facility, nearly hidden beneath a cold metal panel, she spotted it. A small gate meant to guide bags from one belt to another was sticking open just a few inches, almost invisible to the untrained eye. But those few inches were enough to send luggage cascading down the wrong path, jamming one part of the system while starving the rest.

Without hesitation, she had the panel removed and the faulty sensor swapped out. Within minutes, the clogged lines began to flow again, and the backlog melted away. By dawn, the airport was back on track, running smoothly as if nothing had gone wrong.

All because of a tiny, almost invisible glitch and the sharp eyes that caught it before it spiraled further.

A few days later, the airport received her invoice:
Consulting Fee: $60,000

They requested an itemized breakdown.
She replied:

- Replacing the sensor: $300
- Knowing where to look: $59,700

The point?

She didn't redesign the whole system. She didn't chase every alert or overstaff the floor.

She focused on the one critical point that made everything else work.

That's the power of your X Factor.

In your mission, there are dozens of tasks calling for your attention. But not all actions are equal.

Your X Factor is the single activity that unblocks momentum and drives the most progress.

It's the action that, when done consistently, makes everything else flow more smoothly.

Find it. Focus on it. Make it your non-negotiable.

The Trap That Keeps You Stuck

Most people don't fail because they don't care.

They fail because they're busy doing the wrong things.

It's easy to fall into the trap of *false productivity*—endlessly working on what looks important but doesn't move you forward:

- Spending weeks designing a perfect website without landing a single client
- Fine-tuning branding while avoiding outreach
- Researching tools instead of using the ones you already have

These tasks *feel* productive, but they don't create momentum.

The difference? One moves your mission forward. The other just fills time.

When I was writing this book, I had dozens of to-dos: outlining, researching, planning my launch. But none of it would matter without one thing: writing.

My X Factor was clear: sit down and write. No writing, no book.

So, I made writing non-negotiable. Daily sessions. Weekly word count targets. Everything else including marketing, design, launch planning came second. Because if the book didn't exist, none of those things mattered.

Finding Your X Factor: The Three-Question Test

How do you know what your X Factor is? Ask yourself:

- What's the one thing that moves the needle most?
  Not the flashy task. Not the fun distraction.
  The thing that creates progress.
    - Launching a coaching business? It's not the logo, it's coaching clients.
    - Starting a podcast? It's not the mic; it's recording and publishing episodes.

- If I skip this, does everything else fall apart?
  This is your non-negotiable. The thing that gives meaning to all the rest.
  - I could plan this book forever, but if I didn't write, there'd be no book.
  - A trainer can post all day, but if they never train anyone, there's no business.
- Am I making time for it?
  Knowing your X Factor is one thing. Prioritizing it is another.
  - Are you spending time on what works, or just what's easy to cross off the list?
  - Are you moving forward, or just staying busy?

Alex's X Factor: Choosing What Matters Most

After mapping out his goals and building his Mission Blueprint, Alex felt a surge of motivation. He had a clear objective: 10,000 YouTube subscribers in one year, and a plan to reach it. But once he began executing, the path started to blur.

His days quickly filled with busywork.

He read endless articles about YouTube growth hacks.

He spent hours experimenting with logo ideas and obsessing over color palettes.

He even found himself comparing microphones on gear review forums at midnight.

It all felt productive. But deep down, he knew something was off. He wasn't creating. He wasn't publishing. And every week that passed without uploading a new video made the goal feel further away.

One evening, while reviewing his analytics (still mostly empty), he asked himself a simple question:

If I could only do one thing this week to move my channel forward, what would it be?

The answer was obvious: make a video.

That was the moment it clicked.

None of the optimization tricks would matter if there were no content.

His X Factor wasn't designing better thumbnails or building out a brand identity.

It was this: consistently creating and publishing valuable, high-quality videos.

So, he made a shift.

He cleared time on his calendar for filming.

He stopped tweaking his banner design and started scripting episodes.

He treated content creation not as a side task but as the core business of his channel.

The results didn't happen overnight, but they began to take shape.

One video led to the next. His delivery improved. His editing got faster. Comments started coming in; viewers saying things like "This finally makes sense" or "Why didn't anyone explain it like this before?"

By focusing on his X Factor, Alex found momentum.

Not because he cracked some secret algorithm but because he showed up, did the work, and delivered real value week after week.

Your X Factor is Your Shortcut to *Ooh La La*

Many people believe success is about doing more.

The reality?

Success comes from doing fewer things but doing them with total focus.

Your Mission Blueprint gives you direction. Your X Factor is the core gear: the work that turns planning into progress.

When you commit to the right action, everything shifts.

You stop spinning. You start building.

Now, the journey won't always be smooth. Challenges will pop up; some will try to knock you off course, others will open unexpected shortcuts. Let's make sure nothing slows you down. It's time to anticipate what's ahead.

3. POINT C: YOUR CONSTRAINTS

Before filming his first video, Alex made a list.

Not a content list. Not a gear list. A reality check list.

He asked himself:

"What could slow me down?"

"What might speed things up?"

On the left side of the page, he wrote:

- Limited time due to client workload
- Fear of judgment on camera

- Lack of editing experience

On the right, he wrote:

- Experiences explaining finance clearly
- A small but loyal email list
- Support from a videographer friend

That simple ten-minute exercise changed his approach.
He stopped trying to be perfect and started being strategic.
He carved out one protected filming day per week.
He reached out to his friend for editing tips.
He used his email list to test topics before publishing them publicly.
Alex was anticipating the path, so he could navigate it with clarity.

That's what Point C is about: preparing for what might help or hinder you along the way.

Now that you've laid the groundwork by drafting your Mission Blueprint and identifying your X Factor, it's time to add a crucial layer of strategic depth: spotting your risks and accelerators.

In Chapter 3, you mapped out your Point A (where you are now) and Point B (where you want to go). Along the way, we briefly touched on Point C—the constraints that may impact your ability to move forward. These could be time, money, skills, or external conditions.

When you identify these challenges early, you gain the power to navigate them or even turn them into assets.

Strengthening Your Mission Blueprint with the TOWS Strategy

In Chapter 3, you also conducted a SWOT analysis to assess your Strengths, Weaknesses, Opportunities, and Threats. Now, it's time to take those insights further using the TOWS framework—a strategy tool that helps turn obstacles into solutions and strengths into growth accelerators.

Unlike SWOT, which maps where you stand, TOWS flips the lens. It pushes you to create strategies by cross matching your internal traits with external conditions. It forces you to examine how your internal strengths and weaknesses interact with external opportunities and threats, enabling you to craft strategies that mitigate risks and maximize success.

Figure 10 – TOWS Matrix

	Weaknesses	Strengths
Opportunities	**W-O** Strategies *"How can you address weaknesses to leverage an opportunity?"*	**S-O** Strategies *"How can your strengths help you take advantage of opportunities?"*
Threats	**W-T** Strategies *"How can you minimize weaknesses to avoid threats?"*	**S-T** Strategies *"How can you use your strengths to counteract threats?"*

Here's how it works:

1. Create Your TOWS Matrix: Draw a simple 2x2 grid for strengths and weaknesses on one side (columns) and opportunities and threats on the other (rows).
2. Analyze Each Quadrant: Use the four sections of the matrix to create targeted strategies:
   - W-O (Weakness-Opportunity): How can you address weaknesses to leverage an opportunity?
   - S-O (Strength-Opportunity): How can your strengths help you take advantage of opportunities?
   - W-T (Weakness-Threat): How can you minimize weaknesses to avoid threats?
   - S-T (Strength-Threat): How can you use strengths to counteract threats?

Transforming Obstacles into Growth Strategies

Now, let's apply this approach to your journey. Your TOWS analysis is a proofing layer to your action plan.

For example:

- If competition poses a significant threat, how can you capitalize on your unique strengths to differentiate yourself?
- If a lack of marketing experience is a weakness, what opportunity can you pursue to gain the right skills?

This exercise helps you see obstacles in a new light, not as barriers but as opportunities to grow stronger and smarter.

Identifying Risks: The Roadblocks That Could Slow You Down

To manage risk effectively, start by shining a light on the threats that could stall your momentum before they catch you off guard. Consider these common challenges and how they might affect your mission:

Common Risks to Anticipate:

- Market Competition: How will you differentiate yourself? What's your unique value?
- Financial Uncertainty: Do you have a financial safety net or an income strategy to support your venture?
- Self-Doubt & Fear of Failure: Are you mentally prepared to push through inevitable setbacks?
- Time Constraints: Have you structured your schedule to make steady progress without burnout?

Constraints are signposts guiding you to a smarter, more effective approach. Instead of seeing limitations as excuses, use them as the motivation to refine your approach and be even more strategic.

Unleashing Your Accelerators: The Forces That Will Push You Forward

Now that you've identified what could slow you down, it's time to focus on what will speed up your progress. Just like astronauts harness the power of propulsion to break free from gravity, you need key accelerators to propel you forward.

Leverage These Accelerators for Maximum Momentum:

- Smart Tech Tools: Automate tasks, streamline workflows, and use digital platforms to scale your impact without burning out.

- Supportive People: Mentors, peers, and communities offer encouragement, accountability, and insight when you need it most.
- Fast Feedback Loops: Don't wait for perfection. Test early, gather input, and improve as you go.
- Energy Management: Sustainable routines and self-care are fuel for consistent progress.

Sometimes, the very things that seem like constraints can be your biggest accelerators.

For example:

- Limited resources? This forces you to be more creative and scrappy.
- Limited time? This enables you to focus solely on what truly drives progress.
- No experience? This allows you to bring a fresh, unconventional perspective.

Bringing it to life - My TOWS Snapshot

Before we wrap up, I'd like to share a quick snapshot of my own TOWS analysis, specifically from when I was planning the writing of this book.

We didn't delve deeply into my personal SWOT analysis earlier in the journey, but just like you, I took the time to map it out: my strengths, weaknesses, opportunities, and threats. What came next was this: turning that reflection into a strategy using the TOWS framework.

Here's how it mapped out:

- W-O (Weakness–Opportunity):
  Although I had co-written a novel in French with my father years ago, writing a full-length nonfiction book in English, especially one about transformation, was an entirely new challenge. Instead of letting that stop me, I embraced the beginner's mindset. It gave me the freedom to be curious, bend a few rules, and create something fresh and true to my voice.
- S-O (Strength–Opportunity):
  With a foundation in change management, coaching, and leadership, I knew I had the tools to support others through transformation. The opportunity? A growing need for frameworks that are both strategic and human; clear enough to act on but flexible enough to meet

people where they are. This book became the bridge between the two: real tools, a relatable voice, and a mission to help people move forward with confidence.

- W-T (Weakness–Threat):
  Time was a real constraint. With a full plate personally and professionally, it could have easily become a roadblock. Instead, it pushed me to be intentional: to simplify, protect focused time, and let momentum, not pressure, drive the process.

- S-T (Strength–Threat):
  In a crowded space full of self-help and business books, I knew I needed to bring something distinct. That's where the *Ooh La La* concept came in, born from real conversations, and built into a transformational journey. By weaving together structure, authenticity, and a touch of French flair, this book presents a fresh and playful approach to achieving real, lasting change.

Looking back, what felt like risks; time pressure, uncertainty, or inexperience, helped sharpen my thinking and shape the book into something I'm proud of.

So, if your matrix reveals a few messy corners, that's okay. You're not doing it wrong. You're building clarity. And clarity creates momentum.

Now it's your turn.

From Reflection to Action: Locking in Your Strategy

At this stage, your plan is evolving from theory to execution. Take a moment to engage with your TOWS insights and refine your strategy:

- What risks could derail my progress, and how can I counter them?
- Which strengths can I use to seize an opportunity today?
- How can I transform a current weakness into a future strength?
- What is one small step I can take right now to activate my strategy?

You're now equipped to adapt, respond, and accelerate through every twist and turn. Constraints fuel creativity, and when you turn obstacles into accelerators, you become unstoppable.

What's Next?

You've laid out your plan. You've identified your X Factor. You've prepared for risks and found ways to accelerate progress. Now comes the most important part of the journey—YOU.

A great strategy is only as strong as the person executing it. The next chapter is all about investing in yourself; developing the skills, attitude, and habits that will ensure you don't just launch your mission but thrive in it.

Ooh La La success is more than just good planning; it's also about becoming the kind of person who turns plans into reality. Let's take your personal growth to the next level.

OOH *LA LA* HIGHLIGHTS

STEP 5: YOUR LAUNCH PLAN

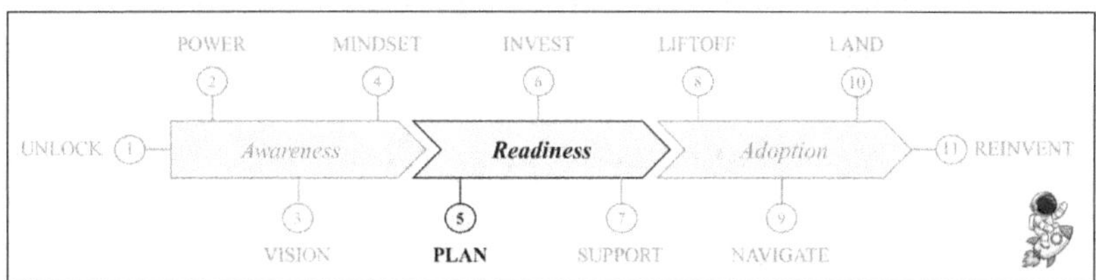

MISSION BRIEF

Your Mission Blueprint is the structured plan that turns bold ideas into tangible results. Without it, even the best ideas remain just dreams. Like an astronaut preparing for launch, your plan must be precise, actionable, and adaptable to ensure progress toward your *Ooh La La* success.

CRITICAL SYSTEMS ANALYSIS

- The Mission Blueprint ensures you stay on course, avoid distractions, and make steady progress.
- The OKR Framework (Objectives & Key Results) provides a simple, high-impact structure:
  - Objective (O) – Your goals on the path to your vision.
  - Key Results (KR) – Measurable milestones proving progress.
  - Key Activities – Specific actions that drive results.
- Your X Factor is the single most impactful action that will drive momentum toward your goal.
  - Success comes from focusing on the right things, not doing everything
  - Avoid the trap of false productivity: being busy isn't the same as making progress.
- Point C: Identifying Risks and Accelerators
  - Anticipating obstacles (e.g., time, skills, market competition) helps you adjust before setbacks occur.

- Leveraging accelerators (e.g., mentors, feedback, technology, and community) speeds up success.
- The TOWS framework builds on your Mission Blueprint like a stress test, pressure-proofing your plan so you're ready for anything the mission throws your way.

PILOT'S REFLECTION

1. Does your plan clearly define objectives, key results, and daily actions? If not, refine your Mission Blueprint.
2. Are you focusing on your X Factor, or getting lost in distractions? What's the one action that will have the most impact?
3. What risks could slow you down? How can you turn them into opportunities for growth?

NEXT COORDINATES

Your plan is set. Now it's time to prepare the pilot, you! In the next chapter, we'll strengthen the skills and habits you need to execute with confidence and lead your mission with impact.

CHAPTER 6

•

INVEST IN YOURSELF

Why Skill-Building and Self-Growth Aren't Optional for Liftoff

A few years ago, I moved to Denver for a new leadership role and quickly realized something important: while I had strong ideas and strategic thinking, my ability to communicate them in front of a room needed serious work.

That's when I discovered Toastmasters.

I walked into that first meeting with a mix of nerves and curiosity. The room was buzzing, people were chatting easily, clearly at home with one another. I wasn't. But then came the "Icebreaker" speech. I stood up, hands gripping the lectern, voice shaking. It was awkward, messy… and completely worth it.

The encouragement I received was immediate and sincere. People smiled, nodded, and gave helpful, thoughtful feedback. I wanted to do better, not because I was pressured to but because I could feel myself growing.

Week by week, I improved.

I learned to pause with purpose, to use gestures intentionally, and to quiet my thoughts enough to speak with clarity. But the real surprise? I started having fun. I entered humorous speech contests. I told stories. I eventually competed at the international level.

Even after moving back to Chicago, I stayed involved. Toastmasters have become more than a skill builder. It was a space for confidence, creativity, and community. It reminded me that learning doesn't have to feel like work. It can be energizing, rewarding, and even joyful.

It taught me a bigger truth: if you want to keep evolving, you must continually upgrade.

Why Your Growth Can't Be Optional

Think about the last time you upgraded your phone. Maybe it was running slowly, couldn't support the latest apps, or the battery drained before noon. Imagine still using an iPhone 5 today, struggling with outdated software, missing out on new features, constantly trying to keep up.

Now apply that same thinking to yourself.

The skills and knowledge that got you this far may not be enough to take you where you want to go next. It's one thing to set big goals but reaching them requires evolving fast enough to keep up. If you don't, you risk getting stuck running old code in a world that's moving forward without you.

Just like astronauts train intensely before liftoff, preparing for your next leap requires intentional upgrades to your capabilities. This chapter is about getting equipped with the right skills, the right learning, and the right approach to level up.

1. BUILDING YOUR SKILL AND KNOWLEDGE INVENTORY

The key is to assess your current skills, identify gaps, and determine what knowledge will be most essential for your success. Think of this as assembling your mission toolbox. Each tool represents a skill or area of expertise that will be critical at different stages of your journey.

Start by conducting a self-assessment:

- What skills do you already have that will help you reach your goal?
- What do you need to learn or improve to remove obstacles?
- Which skills will give you the most significant advantage as you move forward?

Alex's Learning Curve: Becoming a YouTube Financial Educator

Now, let's go back to Alex. While he's highly skilled in finance, starting a content-driven business is a whole new challenge. He now needs an entirely different skill set to succeed.

For Alex, his Skill & Knowledge Inventory might look something like this:

1. Content Creation Skills: Filming, video editing, thumbnail design, and storytelling; all crucial for producing high-quality, engaging content.
2. Public Speaking & Presentation: Translating complex financial concepts into simple, engaging messages that resonate with an online audience.
3. Social Media & Marketing: Understanding YouTube's algorithm, SEO, and engagement strategies to build an audience.
4. Networking & Collaboration: Reaching out to other finance creators, securing guest spots, and building credibility in the community.
5. Monetization Strategies: Exploring ways to generate revenue through ads, sponsorships, and paid content.

Even though Alex has deep expertise in finance, he won't succeed without mastering new skills. That's the challenge we all face when stepping into new territory; the need to constantly upgrade and evolve.

Prioritizing What to Learn First

With so many skills to develop, it's easy to feel overwhelmed. That's why prioritization is key. You don't need to master everything at once; you just need to focus on what will launch you further.

Categorize your skills into three groups:

1. X Factor Skills: The mission-critical skills that directly impact your success. These should be your highest priority.
   - For Alex, this means creating content and engaging in public speaking. Without engaging videos, his channel won't grow, so these must come first.
2. Supportive Skills: Valuable but not essential right away. These enhance progress but can be developed gradually.
   - For Alex, social media marketing is a good fit. It's important, but he can experiment and improve over time.

3. Delegate or Outsource: Skills that aren't worth mastering yourself. If they aren't a core part of your strategy, consider outsourcing or automating them.
   - For Alex, video editing might fall into this category. He could learn the basics but eventually hire an editor to save time.

Taking Action: Learn as You Go

The key is to learn alongside action, not before it. You don't need to be an expert before you start.

Alex isn't going to wait until he's a seasoned public speaker before uploading his first video. And you shouldn't delay executing your plan while trying to master everything in advance.

Your goal is progress, not perfection. As long as you're growing in alignment with your vision, you're on track. Skill-building is not a final goal but an ongoing journey. The more you embrace learning, the more confident and capable you become.

Beyond skills and knowledge lies a key element that separates those who move forward from those who truly thrive. It is the driving force behind resilience, stronger connections, and faster success. In the next section, we will reveal this often-overlooked secret and why it may be the most valuable investment you make.

2. WHY ATTITUDE IS THE GAME-CHANGER

The Carnegie Triangle:

Over a century ago, industrialist Andrew Carnegie sought to uncover the true drivers of success. He commissioned a study that led to an unexpected discovery: technical skills alone do not determine success. Instead, the study revealed what became known as the Carnegie Triangle:

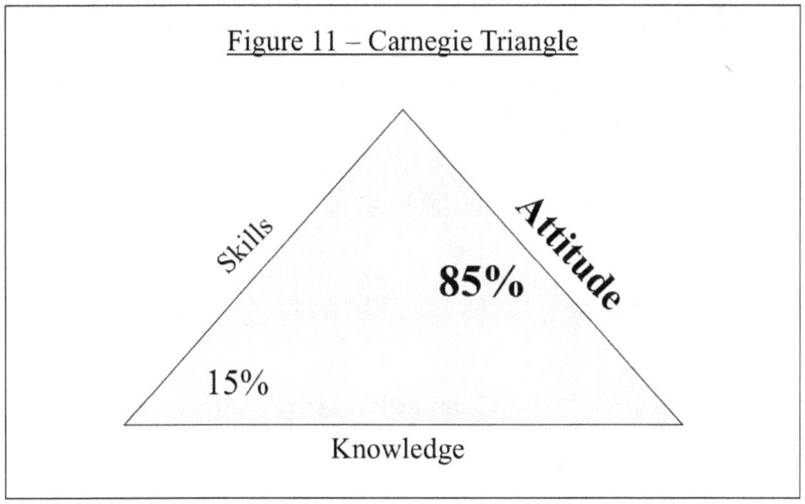

- 85% of success comes from attitude.
- Only 15% comes from technical knowledge and skills.

This overturns conventional wisdom. While skills and knowledge are essential, attitude is the true differentiator. It influences how you show up, how you interact with others, and how you navigate challenges.

Think of it like this: your skills are the rocket's thrusters; they provide the force to move you forward. But attitude is your altitude control system. It determines how high you can climb and whether you stay the course or crash back down. Even with top-tier skills, a poor attitude can keep you stuck on the launchpad.

The Link Between Mindset and Attitude

In Chapter 4, we examined the power of mindset; how your beliefs about growth, failure, and learning influence your ability to succeed. Mindset is internal, it shapes how you view the world and what you believe about your potential.

Attitude is different. It's how you interact with the world based on your mindset. If mindset is the lens you see through, attitude is how you act because of that lens.

For example:

- A growth mindset helps you believe you can improve. But a resilient attitude is what keeps you going when challenges arise.
- A positive mindset lets you see opportunities. But an adaptable attitude is what allows you to pivot when needed.
- A strong mindset sets your internal compass. But a winning attitude determines how you apply it in real life.

Attitude is what people see in you. It's the energy you bring, the way you treat others, and how you handle obstacles. That's why it plays such a massive role in success.

Why Attitude is Your Competitive Advantage

You've seen it before.

- The brilliant developer who's the smartest in the room but can't take feedback without getting defensive.
- The gifted athlete who burns out because they crumble the moment things don't go their way.
- And then there's the newcomer; less polished, maybe, but hungry, open, resilient. They keep showing up, asking questions, and getting better every day.

Guess who rises fastest?

Attitude is the edge. It shapes how you take feedback, how you build trust, and how you respond under pressure. It's what makes some people magnetic to opportunity, while others stall despite their talent.

This isn't just theory. Astronauts, for example, aren't chosen only for their technical mastery. They're trained to stay calm in crisis, adapt quickly, and collaborate without ego, because in space, there's no room for blame or emotional volatility. The same holds in high-stakes environments here on Earth.

If mindset is your internal compass, attitude is how you steer through the real world. It shows up in the way you *adapt* when plans change, extend *empathy* when others disagree, stay optimistic when progress feels slow, keep *showing up* when no one's watching, and *take ownership* when things go wrong. These are signals, and often, they speak louder than expertise.

Without the right attitude, even the strongest mindset stays locked inside your head. Success happens when belief becomes behavior, when what you *think* starts shaping what you do.

So, how do you unlock that shift?

By taking a clear-eyed look at how you're showing up right now.

Let's begin with your Attitude Inventory.

Your Attitude Inventory: Assessing Where You Stand

A few years ago, when I was coaching a high-performing startup team, I ran an exercise that revealed more about their future potential than any strategy session ever could.

We called it an *Attitude Inventory*, and it started with a simple prompt:

"Think of someone you admire—not for what they know but for how they show up."

One team member picked their grandmother, who had led a family through war and resettlement with grace. Another chose Serena Williams. Someone else said, "My old boss, who always kept his cool, even when the servers crashed."

Then I asked them to go deeper: *What exactly makes that person admirable?*

That's when the room shifted. They started naming the invisible qualities that make someone magnetic:

Resilience under pressure. Integrity in tough decisions. A calm confidence that doesn't need to shout. The ability to listen even when it's inconvenient.

These were attitudes traits, and they formed a kind of mirror. Once you name what you admire in others, you start to see where you stand. Let's try it:

Step 1: Identify a Role Model

Picture someone you respect deeply. Ask:

- What do they do under stress?
- How do they treat others when no one's watching?
- What kind of energy do they bring into a room?

Look for qualities like:

- Resilience – Do they bounce back or break down?
- Composure – Do they stay grounded when the pressure rises?
- Empathy – Do they make people feel heard?

- Optimism – Do they focus on what's possible?
- Confidence – Can they lead without needing to dominate?
- Adaptability – Do they flex, or do they freeze?
- Decisiveness – Can they make the hard call without getting stuck?

These qualities are what we often admire most but rarely pause to cultivate in ourselves.

Step 2: Turn the Mirror

After the role model reflection, I had the team answer a few questions, this time pointing inward.

It got quiet.

"When challenges hit, do I lean into problem-solving or spiral into frustration?"

"When someone critiques me, do I grow or get defensive?"

"When I lead, do I bring people with me or just push ahead?"

We called it the *Attitude Dashboard.* Everyone wrote down one strength they were proud of, and one warning light they'd been ignoring. That's where growth begins.

Try it:

- Where do you default to blame instead of ownership?
- When do you resist feedback?
- Where does fear disguise itself as control?

Wherever you feel resistance, that's a growth signal.

Step 3: Make the Shift

Attitude isn't fixed. It's trained. And like muscles, it grows when you put in reps.

In the coaching room, we picked two focus areas per person. Nothing huge. Just the right shifts for that next mission phase. Then we got specific:

- One person started replying to feedback with *"thank you"* even when it stung.
- Another practiced pausing before reacting in meetings.
- A third kept a sticky note with her new motto: *"Be the calmest person in the room."*

They paired those small habits with accountability and reflection. Over time, the shifts were dramatic, not just in how they performed but in how others responded to them.

Attitude is how you show up and if you're willing to look closely at your heroes and yourself, you'll find the levers that make a difference with your success.

Alex's Story: When Attitude Was the Missing Link

Alex had the knowledge built on years of financial expertise. He had the skills; he was learning video production and marketing.

But something was still holding him back.

Despite his best efforts, his channel wasn't growing as expected. It wasn't his lack of expertise or ability; it was his attitude toward the people he was trying to serve that was getting in the way.

Alex struggled with two key attitude challenges:

1. He resisted feedback from his audience. He dismissed negative comments and constructive criticism, assuming that if people didn't immediately resonate with his content, they just didn't "get it." Rather than viewing feedback as a growth opportunity, he perceived it as a personal attack.
2. He wasn't engaging with his community. Alex treated his YouTube channel as a one-way street: he would post a video and move on, without responding to comments or building relationships with his viewers. He focused entirely on what he wanted to share, rather than what his audience needed.

Realizing that his attitude was limiting his ability to connect and grow, Alex decided to make two critical shifts:

1. He embraced feedback as a tool for growth. Instead of ignoring comments, he started asking, "What is my audience trying to tell me? How can I improve?" This shift transformed his content, and he began addressing real concerns, simplifying complex topics, and refining his delivery.
2. He prioritized engagement. Instead of treating his viewers like faceless numbers, he started replying to comments, asking questions, and actively building a community. He developed a habit of responding with enthusiasm and gratitude, even to brutal critiques. This human connection kept people coming back.

These minor attitude adjustments had massive effects:

- His audience felt heard. Instead of talking to his viewers, he started talking with them.
- His content improved. By paying attention to what resonated, he

created more valuable and engaging videos.

- His channel grew because his attitude shift helped him build trust and credibility.

Alex's experience is a reminder that knowledge opens the door, but how you show up is what invites opportunity in.

Whether in business, leadership, or personal growth, the right attitude toward connection, feedback, and service makes all the difference.

Final Thoughts: Attitude Is the Ultimate Accelerator

If your attitude is aligned with success, you move toward *Ooh La La* levels of achievement. But if your attitude is weighing you down, it's like carrying unnecessary baggage into space, slowing progress, and draining energy.

So, ask yourself:

- What kind of attitude will fuel my success?
- How can I make it a daily practice?

What truly shapes your trajectory isn't just what you've learned but how you choose to show up every single day.

The strongest attitude needs the proper foundation; one that keeps your mind and body in peak condition for the journey ahead. And that's precisely where we're headed next.

3. STRONG BODY, STRONG MISSION

"It ain't about how hard you hit. It's about how hard you can get hit and keep moving forward."
– Rocky Balboa

Before Rocky Balboa ever stepped into the ring to face Apollo Creed, he had to prepare, both physically and mentally. He wasn't the most naturally gifted fighter, nor did he have the best resources. But what he did have was unmatched grit and relentless commitment to training.

Rocky's legendary training montage is one of the most iconic sequences in film history. He wakes up before dawn, cracks raw eggs into a glass, and downs them without hesitation. He runs through the streets of Philadelphia, pounding the pavement with determination. He punches slabs of meat in a freezer, trains with unwavering focus, and fights through exhaustion, sweat pouring down his face.

Why? Because he knew that if he wanted to have any chance of beating Apollo, he needed to push himself beyond his limits. He wasn't just preparing for a fight; he was preparing to withstand whatever came his way to keep moving forward, no matter how hard he got hit.

The same applies to your path.

Whatever challenge you're facing; be it launching a business, pursuing a creative project, or making a personal transformation, you must prepare yourself to endure, adapt, and push through obstacles. And just like Rocky, that preparation doesn't start in the moment of battle. It begins long before, in the way you train your body for the mission ahead.

From *Ooh* to *Ooh La La* – The Fitness Edition

If your body is your launch vehicle, then your physical condition determines how far you can go.

> *Ooh* – You feel sluggish. Your energy crashes, your focus is inconsistent, and stress takes a toll on you. Maybe you're running on caffeine and willpower, but it's not sustainable. Your astronaut body is struggling to handle the demands of the mission.
>
> *Ooh La* – You've started making small but meaningful changes. Perhaps you're exercising more regularly, eating healthier, or making sleep a priority. You feel moments of clarity and energy, but they're not fully consistent yet. Your astronaut body is becoming stronger, but it's still adjusting to the rigors of space travel.
>
> *Ooh La La* – Your body is fully mission-ready. You feel energized, clear-headed, and resilient. Exercise fuels you, rather than feeling like a chore; your nutrition supports your performance, and sleep recharges your systems. Your astronaut body is thriving, ready for anything.

The goal is to move from *Ooh* to *Ooh La La*, where your body is an asset, not a liability, in your journey to success.

The Astronaut's Secret: The Body-Mind Connection

Just as Rocky trained relentlessly before stepping into the ring, astronauts undergo grueling physical preparation before heading to space. Their mission demands strength, endurance, and resilience to handle the extreme conditions of space travel.

Without proper conditioning, even the most brilliant astronaut would struggle to function in zero gravity, experience muscle loss, and lack the stamina needed for long missions.

Your journey requires the same holistic approach, because a weak body can slow down even the sharpest mind.

- Movement = Mental Sharpness
  Astronauts train daily to stay strong in space. Regular movement enhances focus, creativity, and problem-solving skills, all of which are essential for success in any endeavor. Even small amounts of movement rewire your brain for better performance.
- Fuel Determines Endurance
  Astronauts don't survive on junk food; they eat for sustained energy and peak performance. You don't need a perfect diet, but the better your fuel, the more stable your energy and focus will be.
- Sleep is Your System Reboot
  In space, poor sleep leads to dangerous errors. On Earth, the same applies. Your body repairs itself, consolidates memory, and strengthens decision-making during sleep. Don't skip this critical system check.

Your body and mind are one system; when they work together, you rise without limits.

Training for Liftoff: Your Rocky-Inspired Plan

You must prepare your body for the demands of your mission.

1. Strength & Endurance: Build Your Physical Power
   - Rocky didn't wake up one day and magically become a champion; he built his endurance through daily training.
   - Move every day: You don't need a gym. Even twenty minutes of walking, strength training, or yoga can improve energy and resilience.

- Train for endurance, not just strength: Incorporate exercises that build long-term stamina, like running, cycling, or circuit training.
- Rocky Mentality: When you feel like quitting, push just a little further. Growth happens at the edge of discomfort.

2. Fuel Like a Champion: Nutrition for Longevity
    - Rocky ate for endurance, power, and peak performance. But let's be real, raw eggs aren't required.
    - Ditch the crash-and-burn cycle: Focus on whole, nutrient-dense foods such as lean proteins, healthy fats, and fiber-rich carbs to keep your energy stable.
    - Hydration is non-negotiable: Dehydration leads to fatigue and brain fog. Drink water like it's part of your training.
    - Consistency over perfection: Just aim for small, consistent upgrades in your diet, not perfection.
3. Recovery & Resilience: Train Smart, Not Just Hard
    One of Rocky's greatest strengths was his ability to take a hit and keep going.
    But no fighter, entrepreneur, leader, or creative can perform at their best without making rest and recovery a priority.
    - Sleep like a champion: The body repairs itself during deep sleep. Aim for 7-9 hours to maximize focus, creativity, and endurance.
    - Listen to your body: Rest days aren't weakness, they're strategy. As with physical fitness, alternating intensity and recovery is key.
    - Mental recovery matters too: High performers train their mental resilience just as much as their physical bodies. Meditation, deep breathing, or even unplugging can help reset your system.

Are You Physically Ready for Liftoff?

You've been working on your mindset, your vision, and your plan but don't forget: your body is the vessel that carries it all.

That doesn't mean you need to be an elite athlete before launching, far from it. But to show up fully for your goals, you need the energy, focus, and resilience to sustain the journey.

So, ask yourself:

- Are you building the stamina to stay consistent when things get tough?

- Are you fueling your body in a way that supports clarity and creativity?
- Are you giving yourself space to recover so you don't burn out before liftoff?

Think of this as your training montage, building your foundation one small habit at a time. A brisk walk, a nourishing breakfast, a few extra minutes of sleep you once gave up to scrolling. These are small actions but fuel your momentum.

Treat your body as the vital support system it is, not something to fix before launch but something to strengthen along the journey.

Speaking of launching, do you have to do it alone?

In the next chapter, we will focus on assembling your crew, mentors, allies, and champions who will keep you on course, help you push through resistance, and celebrate every victory.

Your launch window is coming soon. Let us make sure you are fully supported when it opens.

OOH *LA LA* HIGHLIGHTS

STEP 6: INVEST IN YOURSELF

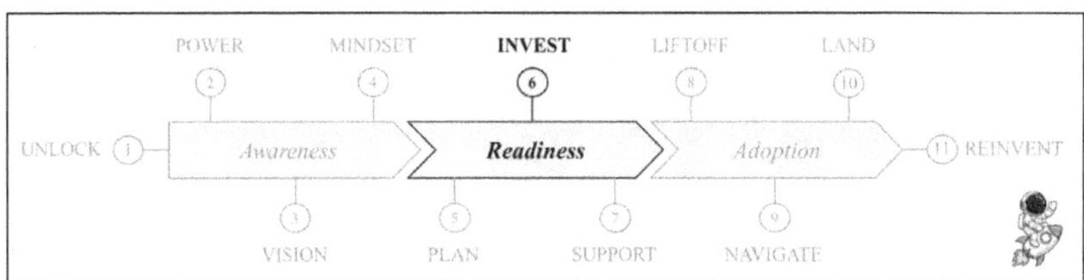

MISSION BRIEF

Just like astronauts train extensively before a mission, achieving success requires continuous self-investment. The skills, knowledge, and attitude that got you here won't necessarily take you to the next level. To reach *Ooh La La* success, you must upgrade yourself; learning what matters most, sharpening your attitude, and strengthening your body to sustain long-term progress.

CRITICAL SYSTEMS ANALYSIS

- Skill & Knowledge Inventory – Assess what you know, what you need to learn, and what will have the biggest impact.
- Prioritize:
    - X Factor Skills – The essential skills that will directly influence your success.
    - Supportive Skills – Useful but not essential right away. Develop gradually.
    - Delegate/Outsource – Low-priority tasks that don't require your expertise.
- Learn as You Go – Growth is born from experience, not from having it all figured out beforehand
- Attitude as Your Competitive Advantage
    - Carnegie Triangle: 85% of success comes from attitude and people skills, not just technical expertise.
    - Mindset vs. Attitude: Mindset shapes your beliefs, but attitude determines how you show up and apply them.

  - Winning Attitude Traits: Resilience, composure, empathy, optimism, confidence, adaptability, and decisiveness—these set successful people apart.
- Strong Body, Strong Mission
  - Movement = Mental Clarity – Regular exercise boosts focus, creativity, and stamina.
  - Fuel for Performance – Proper nutrition ensures sustained energy and cognitive sharpness.
  - Recovery is Non-Negotiable – Quality sleep and stress management keep your systems running optimally.

PILOT'S REFLECTION

1. What key skills do I need to develop to advance to the next level?
2. Is my attitude elevating my success or holding me back?
3. Am I prioritizing my physical health to sustain long-term performance?

NEXT COORDINATES

You're trained and ready! Next, we'll build your support system to help you sustain momentum and navigate the challenges ahead.

CHAPTER 7

•

BUILDING YOUR SUPPORT SYSTEM

1. THE POWER OF LEVERAGE

Greek philosopher Archimedes famously said, *"Give me a lever long enough and a place to stand, and I will move the world."*

He was talking about physics, but this idea is equally powerful when applied to success. No one achieves greatness alone. Leverage is what allows us to accomplish far more than we ever could on our own.

Leverage in Action: How This Book Was Built

Before I finished writing the first part of the book, I hired a social media manager.

That might sound backward, but I knew that if I wanted this book to make an impact, I'd need a platform. And if I tried to build one while also writing 50,000 words? Frankly, the book would never get finished. So, while I focused on writing, she focused on building. She created a content calendar, shared my ideas with the world, and helped me grow a following before the book even existed.

That freed me up to focus on the messy, beautiful work of getting words onto the page.

Soon after, I brought in a handful of trusted beta readers; real people who could tell me, *"This part confused me,"* or *"I loved this chapter—more of this!"* They helped keep me on track, catching blind spots before they became bad habits. Their feedback was early fuel; it gave me the confidence to keep going and the clarity to pivot when something wasn't working.

Once the draft was solid, I handed it off to my editor. Or rather, editors, plural. One helped shape the flow, ensuring the story arc guided the reader smoothly from start to finish. Another zeroed in on the language, tightening every sentence, cutting what didn't serve, elevating what did. What I thought was "done" got sharper, stronger, and far more readable.

Then came the visuals.

I once tried to design the book cover myself. Honestly, I think even my printer was embarrassed to produce it. So, I called in a designer. I gave her a few vague notes: "clean but bold, minimalist but inviting," and somehow, she brought the exact vision to life. When she sent over the final mock-up, I literally said out loud, "*Ooh La La*. That's it."

Next, I worked with a book layout specialist, someone who turned my Word document into a beautifully structured interior. Every page, every margin, every heading was carefully crafted. The book finally looked the way it felt.

Then came the website. I needed a place to bring everything together: a digital home where people could find the book, connect with me, and explore deeper. So, I called in a web designer, and just like the rest of the team, she took my scrambled thoughts and turned them into something professional, clear, and aligned with the message.

And all along the way, I leaned on people I trusted—friends, past clients, and mentors—each one offering insights and wisdom that shaped the content. A question from a coaching call. A story someone told me over coffee. A phrase that stuck in a workshop. These were the building blocks.

Truthfully, this book was never a solo project. It was a team effort, layered with expertise, feedback, creativity, and generosity.

This book didn't just get written; it got built. And the same approach can build whatever you're dreaming of.

That's the power of leverage. It's about focusing on your key activities while letting the right people help with the rest. It means tapping into the right minds, tools, and support systems so you can focus on the mission-critical work only you can do.

When you stop trying to do everything alone, you go further, faster, and with a lot more joy.

Let's break down seven powerful ways to use leverage, so you can dodge asteroids, and keep your momentum going.

Harnessing the Seven Forms of Leverage

1. Other People's Energy – Freeing Up Your Time for What Matters

Highly successful people don't do everything themselves, instead they focus on their highest-value tasks and delegate the rest.

When writing this book, I could have spent hours figuring out how to format each chapter, create a marketing plan, or schedule social media posts. But instead, I leveraged others' energy so I could focus on the core task: writing.

Ask yourself:

- What's draining your time that someone else could do better or faster?
- What's keeping you from focusing on your X Factor (as we covered in Chapter 5)?

Ooh La La Tip: The fastest way to accelerate your success is to stop doing everything yourself.

2. Other People's Knowledge – Learning Smarter, Not Harder

Instead of spending years figuring things out the hard way, leverage the wisdom of those who have already been there.

My daughter and I are learning to play golf. Instead of hacking away at the driving range, guessing what we were doing wrong, we hired a coach to guide us. He immediately spotted areas where we could improve: posture, grip, and swing technique. What would have taken years to learn through trial and error became clear within a few lessons.

The same applies to any goal:

- Want to start a business? Follow entrepreneurs who've done it.
- Want to master a skill? Find someone who has already cracked the code.
- Want to grow an audience? Study what works instead of guessing.

You don't have to start from scratch; borrow brilliance from those who already figured it out.

3. Other People's Money – Fueling Growth Without Waiting Forever

Success often requires resources, and relying only on your funds can be limiting.

Think about Marie, whose journey we explored in Part I. She dreamed of opening a holistic wellness center but didn't have the funds to get started. Instead of waiting years to save up, she sought an investor who believed in her vision. That financial backing allowed her to launch her dream sooner and start making an immediate impact on lives.

Even smaller amounts of other people's money can accelerate your progress. It could be a short-term loan from a supporter to fund a critical piece of equipment, or a small stake from a partner who believes in your vision. The goal is to use outside funds strategically, not to take on reckless debt but to create momentum you couldn't achieve as quickly on your own.

Ooh La La Tip: Smart people invest in themselves. The question isn't "Can I afford it?" but "What's the cost of not doing it?"

4. Other People's Success – Reverse-Engineering What Works

Every successful person left clues. Instead of guessing, study how they got there.

For this book, I didn't just write what sounded good, I studied authors, business leaders, and creators to see what worked. By reverse-engineering their process, I avoided years of trial and error.

The same applies to any goal. Want to grow on YouTube? Study successful channels. Want to launch a product? Analyze top-performing brands. The roadmap already exists. Just learn from it.

5. Other People's Failures – Learning Without the Pain

Failures are costly lessons but here's the good news: you don't have to pay for them all yourself.

Alex, from our earlier chapters, studied other YouTubers who had struggled to grow. He noticed patterns; what worked and what didn't. He noticed that channels that frequently failed often lacked consistency, had weak audience engagement, or failed to adhere to SEO best practices.

By learning from their mistakes, he sidestepped common pitfalls and built his channel faster than if he had tried to figure it all out alone.

6. Other People's Ideas – Expanding Your Perspective

You may not have original ideas right away; however, you can borrow and combine the right ones.

- Apple didn't invent the MP3 player—they just made it better.

- Netflix didn't invent streaming—they refined it into a winning model.
- Amazon didn't invent e-commerce—they mastered the logistics.

In the same way, pay attention to the ideas around you. The next significant breakthrough on your journey may come from a conversation, a book, or even an unrelated industry. Keep your radar on.

7. Other People's Contacts – Unlocking Hidden Opportunities

Let's make this one about you.

- Do you know someone who has connections in your industry?
- Who do you know that can introduce you to the right people?
- Is there a mentor, colleague, or acquaintance who could introduce you to an investor, a partner, or an opportunity?
- Are you actively building relationships, or are you waiting for luck to strike?

What you know sets the foundation, who you know builds the bridge. One well-placed introduction can change everything. A mentor, a business partner, a key investor, or a media opportunity could all come through a single connection.

Bringing It All Together – The *Ooh La La* Effect

Leverage is your success multiplier. When you stop trying to do everything alone and start tapping into the right resources, success comes faster, smoother, and with far less stress.

So, as you move forward, ask yourself:

- Where am I trying to "do it alone" when I should be leveraging help?
- Which of these seven types of leverage can I use right now?
- What's one action I can take today to maximize my momentum?

The most successful people are the ones who leverage the smartest, not necessarily the ones who work the hardest.

Your mission? Find your levers, fuel your launch, and move the world without burning out in orbit.

2. ASSEMBLING YOUR CREW

In the last section, we explored the power of leverage; how tapping into other people's knowledge, expertise, and resources can accelerate your progress.

Yes, leverage means getting value from others, but it also means building a team that strengthens and supports your mission.

Even the most skilled and determined astronauts do not launch alone. Behind every successful mission is a dedicated crew: mentors, specialists, peers, and personal supporters, each playing a key role in making sure every phase of the journey runs smoothly.

Your success depends on the crew you assemble. Who's guiding you? Who's supporting you? Who's helping you fill the gaps? It's time to make sure your mission is fully staffed with the right people.

Here are four types of crew members you'll need on your mission:

1. Mission Control: Your Mentors and Advisors

Every space mission needs ground control; the calm, experienced voices who help navigate uncertainty and keep things aligned when you're deep in the chaos. Your mentors and advisors play that role in your journey.

One of mine gave me a piece of advice I'll never forget. I was drowning in early feedback from beta readers, contradictory opinions, well-meaning suggestions, and a growing feeling that I might be writing this book for everyone except myself. He said:

"This is your book. You'll receive tons of feedback, but ultimately, you make the call. You won't please everyone, and you're not supposed to."

That instantly re-centered me. Mentors help you zoom out. They remind you what matters.

If you don't have that kind of voice in your corner yet, start small. Send a thoughtful question to someone you admire. You might be one honest conversation away from clarity.

2. Fellow Astronauts: Peers Who Share the Journey

Astronauts don't fly alone, they train in squads, prepare as a unit, and lean on each other in the hardest moments. That kind of camaraderie matters in your mission, too.

I was lucky to have a few friends going through a parallel journey, working or running their businesses *and* trying to write a book at the same time.

We weren't critiquing each other's chapters or workshopping titles. We were swapping voice notes about how hard it was to stay consistent and how writing sessions kept getting pushed aside for "real work." That shared experience, that connection of being at the same stage, facing the same struggles, meant everything. It reminded me I wasn't behind or broken. I was simply in the messy middle, surrounded by good company.

If you're not yet surrounded by people like this, it's time to build your circle. Look into mastermind groups, join niche communities, attend local meetups, or even start one yourself.

3. Specialists: The Engineers and Technicians Who Keep Things Running

No astronaut is expected to know everything. That's why missions include engineers, analysts, and technical experts who keep everything working behind the scenes.

You'll need that, too.

You might be the visionary, but that doesn't mean you should handle every detail alone. Specialists, people with focused expertise, can help you move faster, smarter, and with less stress.

Take Alex. As he grew his YouTube channel, he knew content was his strength, but branding, editing, and promotion? Not so much. So, he brought in:

- A video editor to ensure his content looked polished and professional.
- A graphic designer to create compelling thumbnails that increase engagement.
- A social media strategist to help him optimize his reach.

By leveraging the expertise of specialists, Alex freed up his time to focus on his core strength: creating high-quality financial content.

Where do you need specialists in your journey? Whether it's hiring an expert, delegating tasks, or collaborating with someone who has strengths where you don't, build a team that supports your weaknesses so you can focus on what you do best.

4. Your Inner Circle: The People Who Keep You Going

This part of your crew is less about business and more about belief.

Behind every bold mission is a quiet, consistent kind of support—partners, family, close friends—people who see your potential and remind you of it when you forget.

These people may not understand all the technical aspects of your dream, but they show up in ways that matter: cheering for you, listening without judgment, or simply reminding you to take a break.

When I was writing, I wasn't doing it alone. I had people behind the scenes encouraging me, offering feedback, or simply reminding me that it mattered. That emotional fuel kept me going when the days got long.

So, who's in your inner circle? Who brings you back to center when things feel chaotic? Ensure that these relationships are nurtured as intentionally as any other strategy.

Clarify Roles and Set Expectations

Once your crew is forming, it's time to define the roles. Who's helping you with what? When will you connect? How will you collaborate?

You don't need a formal structure, but even casual support systems thrive when there's clarity.

Ask yourself:

- What kind of support do I need most right now?
- Who in my world could offer that support or whom do I need to seek out?
- How can I maintain the connection? Is it weekly check-ins, monthly chats, or quick texts of encouragement?

Just like a launch team needs to know their duties and timing, your crew needs to understand how they contribute. That's how you create aligned momentum.

The Final Push: Is Your Crew *Ooh, Ooh La,* or *Ooh La La?*

Now that you've thought about assembling your crew, take a moment to assess where you stand:

- *Ooh*: You're flying solo, figuring everything out alone. It's exhausting, and progress is slow. You are handling every decision and every challenge by yourself, and it's starting to feel overwhelming.
- *Ooh La*: You have some support, but gaps remain. You're making progress, but you know you could move faster with the right people in your corner. There are still areas where you're stretched thin.

- *Ooh La La*: You have mentors, peers, specialists, and supporters all working together to fuel your mission. The momentum is real, and with every step forward, you feel the power of a strong, aligned crew.

Ask yourself:

- Who do I still need to reach out to?
- What's one connection I can strengthen this week?
- What role am I trying to play that someone else could do better?

With the right people beside you, your odds of success increase exponentially, and the journey becomes a lot more meaningful (and fun).

And once your crew is in place...

3. FINAL SYSTEMS CHECK

Before liftoff, Mission Control conducts a final Go/No-Go Systems Check, verifying every critical system, assessing risks, and confirming full crew alignment. If any major system isn't ready, the launch is delayed. But if everything checks out, it's time to ignite the engines.

Right now, you're at that moment.

In Chapter 5, you designed your launch plan, in Chapter 6, you identified key investments in yourself, and in Chapter 7, you started to build your support network.

Now, it's time for your final readiness check.

The Go/No-Go Checklist: Are You Ready to Launch?

- Mission Blueprint Ready – Do you have a clear goal, measurable milestones, and high-impact activities mapped out?
- X Factor Identified – Have you identified the one key action that will generate the most momentum?
- Risks and Accelerators Assessed – Have you considered potential constraints and identified the forces that will accelerate your journey?
- Strategic Investments Identified – Have you mapped out what you need to invest in along the way, whether it's new skills, tools,

coaching, or resources? Some of these investments won't happen on the ground; they'll be mid-flight adjustments.

- Leverage Plan in Motion – Have you identified what and who you will leverage to maximize efficiency, whether it's knowledge, networks, expertise, or resources? Some forms of leverage will happen pre-launch, while others will become available as you gain altitude.

- Crew in Place – Have you surrounded yourself with the right mentors, peers, and specialists who will support and challenge you?

If you can confidently check off most of these, congratulations, you're Go for Launch!

But What If You're Hesitating?

Maybe you feel like you don't have everything figured out yet. Maybe your support system isn't as strong as you'd like it to be. Perhaps you're waiting for the moment when everything feels perfect.

Here's what I've learned: You'll never feel 100 percent ready. Even astronauts after years of training feel the weight of uncertainty before liftoff. But action creates momentum, and momentum builds confidence.

You don't need all the answers before launching. Some of your biggest lessons, investments, and adjustments happen mid-flight once you're already moving.

If you've made it this far, you've already weighed your options. The next step is to commit. Because once the engines ignite, hesitation fades away.

The *Ooh La La* Scale: Where Are You?

Let's take a quick self-assessment. Where do you stand on the launch readiness scale?

- *Ooh*: You're circling in pre-launch holding—checking every detail, questioning your readiness. Analysis paralysis is keeping you grounded.

- *Ooh La*: You've completed most systems checks, and you're on the launch pad. But doubts linger; do you need another go-around, or is it time to commit?

- *Ooh La La*: The countdown has started. You know the mission won't be perfect, but you've trained, prepared, and accepted that some adjustments will happen mid-flight. There's only one thing left to do: launch.

Now, ask yourself: What's the next step to move you toward *Ooh La La*?

- If you're in *Ooh* – What's the one Go for Launch decision you need to make today? What's a small action that will get the engines warming up?
- If you're in *Ooh La* – What's the last systems check? Do you need a final investment, a key resource, or a confidence boost from Mission Control? What would make you give that final "Go" call?
- If you're in *Ooh La La* – There's nothing left but the countdown. You've run through the final checklist. The engines are primed. You trust your preparation. It's time.

The Final Countdown:

At this stage, the rocket is fully fueled, the launch sequence is locked in, and Mission Control is running through the final Go/No-Go poll:

✓ Mission Clarity? Go.

✓ Momentum Strategy? Go.

✓ Risk Management? Go.

✓ Resource Alignment? Go.

✓ Support Systems? Go.

✓ Mindset Locked In? Go.

✓ You? … Go or No-Go?

The launch window is open. The hesitation window is closing.
You've done the work. You've built the plan. You've assembled the proper support.

No more waiting.
T-minus 10… 9… 8…
This is it.
7… 6… 5…
Your mission is calling.
4… 3… 2… 1…
Ignition.

Liftoff… Welcome to Part III.

OOH LA LA HIGHLIGHTS

STEP 7: BUILD YOUR SUPPORT SYSTEM

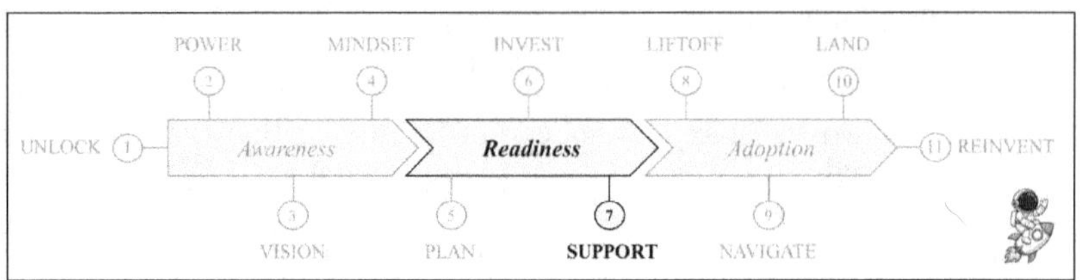

MISSION BRIEF

No astronaut launches alone. Behind every successful mission is a dedicated crew—mentors, peers, specialists, and supporters—who provide guidance, expertise, and accountability. Leverage is the key to multiplying your success, allowing you to work smarter, not harder.

When you tap into the right networks, knowledge, and resources, you accelerate your journey and avoid needless struggle.

CRITICAL SYSTEMS ANALYSIS

- The seven forms of leverage help maximize results with minimal resistance:
  1. Other People's Energy – Delegate tasks so you can focus on your highest-value work.
  2. Other People's Knowledge – Learn from experts instead of struggling through trial and error.
  3. Other People's Money – Strategic investments can fast-track your progress.
  4. Other People's Success – Reverse-engineer what works instead of reinventing the wheel.
  5. Other People's Failures – Study mistakes to avoid costly setbacks.
  6. Other People's Ideas – Expand your perspective by borrowing and refining great concepts.
  7. Other People's Contacts – One introduction can open life-changing opportunities.

- Building your crew is equally important:
    - Mission Control (Mentors & Advisors) – Guides who provide wisdom, perspective, and expertise.
    - Fellow Astronauts (Peers & Accountability Partners) – A support network that challenges and uplifts you.
    - Specialists (Experts & Technicians) – People who fill in the gaps where you lack expertise.
    - Inner Circle (Personal Support System) – Friends and family who offer encouragement and resilience.

PILOT'S REFLECTION

1. Are you trying to do everything alone instead of leveraging others' strengths?
2. Do you have a strong enough crew—mentors, peers, and specialists—to support your journey?
3. What's one relationship you can strengthen or one connection you can make this week to enhance your mission?

NEXT COORDINATES

Preparation is done. Now it's time for action. In Part III, we shift from preparation to execution. The mission is a go; it's time to lift off.

PART III

•

Adoption

Lift Off into Action

CHAPTER 8: LIFTOFF

•

YOU ARE IN THE DRIVER'S SEAT!

1. THE POWER OF ACTION

"And we have liftoff!"

The engines are roaring. The ground is shaking. There's no turning back now.

In the last chapter, your countdown began. You prepared, checked systems, assessed risks, built support, and gathered what you need to propel forward. And now? You've launched.

At this moment, hesitation is gone. The force of liftoff is stronger than the gravity that once held you in place. This is the power of action, when all the preparation, strategy, and thinking transform into doing.

There's a distinct moment in every great endeavor when you cross the threshold between thinking about something and doing it. That moment is exhilarating. It's terrifying.

And it changes everything.

What Action Feels Like

For me, that moment happened on Saturday, November 16, 2024.

I'd been circling this idea for years. *Ooh La La* had been bouncing around in my head like a catchy song I couldn't shake. But I couldn't quite figure out what it was. A podcast? A coaching framework? A workshop series? Maybe all of them? I wasn't sure.

Then, in the summer of 2024, clarity struck: *This wasn't just an idea.* It was a book, a roadmap to help people move from being stuck in overthinking to taking meaningful action. Not just talking about their goals but doing the things that bring them to life.

From July to November, I went all in. I mapped out the book's flow, pieced together stories, and created exercises I knew would help people make real progress. And, because I love a good prep session (read: I tend to overcomplicate things when I'm excited), I spent hours fine-tuning the concept... but not writing.

Instead, I buried myself in everything but the words. Researching marketing strategies. Debating cover designs. Even curating a launch party playlist, because obviously, you can't write a transformational book without the perfect soundtrack. I told myself I needed the whole journey mapped before I could take the first step.

Then came my wake-up call.

I set a deadline: December 2025. That's when the book would be out, at the latest. No more circling. No more "I'll start when I feel ready." Just writing.

I worked backward from that date, set key milestones, and locked in my X Factor—the single most important action that would move me forward: putting words on the page.

And on November 16, 2024, I did the one thing I'd been avoiding for months. I opened a blank document and started typing.

It felt clunky at first, like trying to do a push-up after skipping arm day for weeks. The words didn't flow. I second-guessed every sentence. But something shifted as I kept going. The hesitation faded. I wasn't thinking about writing anymore. I was writing.

That was my liftoff moment.

Every journey has this moment:

- The moment a creator uploads their first YouTube video.
- The moment an entrepreneur nervously dials their first potential client.
- The moment someone signs up for the race, books the plane ticket, or walks into their first big meeting.

It's the moment when you stop waiting for the perfect conditions and just start.

And that? That's when everything changes.

Why Action Trumps Perfection

Perfection is a seductive illusion. It whispers, 'Wait until you're ready,' like a siren luring ships into still waters. But waiting is a trap.

Clarity doesn't come before action; it comes from action.

Think about the astronauts. They don't wait until they feel ready to launch into space. They prepare as best they can, but at some point, they commit. They trust their preparation and move forward, knowing they'll adjust along the way.

The same applies to your goal.

- You don't need the perfect business plan to start your business.
- You don't need to know every detail to begin writing your book.
- You don't need complete confidence to step onto the stage and give your first talk.

Progress happens in motion.

Momentum compounds. Small actions lead to bigger actions.

- One sentence becomes a paragraph, which in turn becomes a chapter.
- One client turns into a business.
- One video turns into a channel.

Getting it done is better than getting it perfect. You can polish a draft, refine a business, and sharpen a skill, but you cannot improve what does not exist.

You've launched; now the goal is to stay on course. Let's explore the laws that quietly shape your trajectory and determine how far you'll go.

2. THE LAWS OF THE UNIVERSE

Imagine standing at the base of a rocket launch site. The engines rumble beneath you. The countdown echoes across the concrete.

No one improvises a launch. Astronauts don't cross their fingers and "hope it works."

They lift off by yielding to forces greater than themselves, including gravity, velocity, and aerodynamics.

They *master* the laws that shape the skies, then use them to go higher.

Success on Earth works the same way.

There are invisible principles at play; powerful, consistent, and non-negotiable. You can't see them, but they shape every outcome.

When you align with these laws, progress feels natural. When you ignore them, everything feels like an uphill grind.

Let's look at three of the most influential ones. These laws act like rocket fuel. Each one builds on the last, helping you turn intention into momentum and momentum into results.

1. The Law of Vibration: You Attract What You Expect

Every thought you think, and every emotion you feel, sends out a signal. Like a radio tower, your mindset broadcasts a frequency.

When you're filled with doubt or hesitation, you radiate mixed signals. And the world mirrors that back to you: unclear responses, shaky opportunities, dead ends.

However, when you operate from clarity, belief, and purpose, things start to fall into place. People respond. Doors open. You meet the right contacts, stumble on the right idea, and find yourself in the right room.

It might look mystical from the outside, but it's really just focus, your internal state shaping your external outcomes.

To shift your reality, shift your expectations. Instead of saying, "I hope this works," say:

- "This is happening."
- "I'm all in."
- "This is who I am now."

The clearer your signal, the stronger your results will be.

2. The Law of Action: Alignment Creates Momentum

Mindset sets the tone but movement sets things in motion.

You won't manifest success by thinking about it. You have to do something. Take steps. Experiment. Speak up. Show up.

But not just any movement; *aligned* movement.

Busywork won't get you there. But brave, relevant action will.

- Want to be a writer? Write.
- Want to be a coach? Coach someone, anyone.
- Want to be a speaker? Speak, even if it's to five people in a library basement.

Momentum doesn't come from waiting. It comes from starting.

Action tells the universe you're serious and that signal gets returned.

3. The Law of Compensation: Value = Rewards

Vibration sets your direction.

Action creates motion.

Compensation is the feedback loop.

The more value you create for others, the more the world responds, with attention, trust, opportunity, income, and impact:

- The creator who shares insight earns an audience.
- The entrepreneur who solves real problems earns loyalty.
- The leader who elevates others earns influence.

Ask yourself:

- How can I serve at a higher level?
- What result am I helping someone achieve?
- How can I make something that truly matters?

The more you grow, the more you can give.

The more you give, the more you're rewarded.

Bringing It All Together

When you align your mindset (Vibration), take meaningful steps (Action), and consistently deliver value (Compensation), success becomes less about striving and more about flow.

Work with these laws, and you don't have to push so hard.

You'll move with momentum.

When you do, the universe moves with you.

Time for one more law? The Law of Authenticity

Now, before we move on, I have one more law to introduce. It's not technically a universal law, but if it were up to me, it would be. Since I can't rewrite the physics of the universe, I'll do the next best thing: introduce you to an *Ooh La La* Law I call The Law of Authenticity.

This one isn't about vibration, action, or compensation. It's about bringing your whole self to the table, because you can't expect extraordinary results if you're only showing up as half of who you are.

Remember earlier in the book when I shared one of my favorite quotes? *"Be yourself; everyone else is already taken."* – Oscar Wilde.

Consider this your official permission slip to embrace that idea fully. It's important to take action, but *who* is taking that action determines how far you'll go. If you're holding parts of yourself back, you're flying with limited power.

Carla Harris, a Wall Street executive, leadership speaker, and gospel singer, once shared a powerful lesson. For years, she kept her love for singing separate from her corporate career, convinced that to be taken seriously in finance, she had to hide that part of herself. Then one day, she began sharing her passion for music. Everything shifted. Clients connected with her on a deeper level, seeing her as more than just another banker. They saw her. That connection built trust, opened doors, and made her stand out.

As she put it:
"No one can be you as well as you can be you. Never submerge what is uniquely you."

The lesson? The things that make you different aren't distractions, they're assets.

What Are You Holding Back?

So, let me ask: What are the parts of yourself that you're keeping in the shadows?

Are you trying to fit into a mold instead of standing out with what makes you unique?

I'll admit, I used to think being "professional" meant only presenting the polished, neatly packaged version of myself. But over time, I realized every piece of who I am contributes to my success in ways I never expected.

For me? Well, here's the full, unfiltered version.

I'm French, so yes, I have opinions about cheese, wine, bread, and how coffee should be consumed (hint: lukewarm, over-sugared gas station coffee is an insult to humanity). I golf, badly, but I try. I love to write, whether it's a card, a speech, or a book (which is probably obvious by now).

I get ridiculously excited when people see paths to growth whether it's in business, life, or that lightbulb moment when they realize, "Wait… I can do this!"

I coach, I consult, and I listen to punk rock music, which, admittedly, surprises people when they find out I also enjoy a well-paired wine and a beautifully plated meal.

Speaking of food, I'm a hardcore foodie. I don't just love eating; I love the entire experience. The planning, the sourcing, the slow process of creating something incredible in the kitchen. And don't even get me started on travel; I could spend months happily buried in flight options, itinerary hacks, and discovering the one hidden café in a random European town that serves the best croissants known to mankind.

Then there's the creative, builder side of me. I thrive on building things from scratch. A book? Yes. A business? Absolutely. But also… a vegetable garden with cute paths and wood fences. A flower garden with a retention wall (which, I should note, is still standing, so clearly, I did something right). A brick surround for my grill area that makes me feel like some backyard BBQ architect. Oh, and my DIY retractable golf simulator suite in my garage, because why not turn a parking space into a personal driving range?

And you know what? All of these things make me who I am.

Each piece plays a role in how I connect with people. And that's the thing; you never know which part of you will open a door.

Authenticity builds trust. It's what makes you stand out in a world full of sameness. And, in the grand equation of success, being yourself is your competitive advantage.

So, tell me, what's the version of you that you haven't fully let the world see yet? Because odds are, that's where the magic is.

Are You Ready to Keep Going?

You're past the launchpad. You're moving. And now? It's about staying in motion.

The biggest mistake people make after liftoff is thinking the hardest part is over. But space travel doesn't work like that: once you're in motion, you have to navigate, adjust, and course-correct in real time.

This next phase is about mastering that process. How do you track progress? How do you stay disciplined? How do you know when to pivot and when to push harder?

That's exactly what we're diving into next.

3. ASSESSING PERFORMANCE

This section is about assessing, tracking, and adapting. And just as we're evaluating progress, let's quickly revisit how our story has unfolded so far.

In Part I, Marie left her corporate job to start a wellness center, driven by a clear desire for change and the courage to take her first steps.

In Part II, Alex, a financial expert, prepared to launch his YouTube channel with a structured plan, clear milestones, and the right support.

Now, in Part III, we enter the execution phase where strategy meets reality, challenges appear, and adaptability becomes the deciding factor between growth and stagnation.

You'll still hear from Marie and Alex, but they'll be joined by others, like Sophie, a design consultant who discovered how discipline and tracking the right indicators could fuel sustainable growth; Leo, an artist who came face-to-face with the kind of challenges that almost made him quit, but didn't; and Emma, a business owner who finally found a way to break through years of plateau to create new momentum in her company.

Expect fresh stories, new challenges, and powerful lessons that show execution as the dynamic, ever-changing process it truly is.

Ready to see what it really takes to bring a vision to life? Let's begin.

A Tragic Miscalculation

Now, I know this might feel like a shift in tone, and I promise no harm is intended. But bear with me for a moment, because it's a powerful point.

In 1979, a passenger jet left New Zealand for a sightseeing flight over Antarctica. What the crew didn't know was that their flight path coordinates had been entered just two degrees off.

That tiny error?

It put the plane twenty-eight miles east of its intended path, straight into the side of Mount Erebus. Everyone on board was lost.

Two degrees. That's all it took.

It's a haunting example but a powerful one: small misalignments, left unchecked, become massive course corrections, or worse, full-on collisions.

That's why astronauts don't just launch and hope.

They constantly monitor data:

- Speed – Are we moving at the right pace?
- Trajectory – Are we still heading toward the target?

- Fuel levels – Are we using our energy wisely?
- External conditions – What's shifting around us?

Success in space and life depends on feedback.

Tracking is how you stay on course. Without it, even the best plan becomes guesswork.

And it's the same with your goals: if you don't measure progress, you start to drift. You lose momentum. Worst of all, you won't realize you're off track until you're miles from where you meant to be.

A mission without tracking is just a hopeful experiment.

And *Ooh La La* success? That's not accidental.

That's intentional: by design, by attention, by course correction.

Connecting Back to Chapter 5: The Bridge Between Planning and Execution

Back in Chapter 5, we introduced the OKR framework—Objectives and Key Results—to help you structure your goals.

Let's do a quick refresher:

- Objective – What success looks like on the path toward that vision.
- Key Results – The measurable milestones that show progress.
- Key Activities – The specific actions that get you there.

At that stage, you identified your X Factor, the one action that would have the biggest impact on your success.

Now that you're in execution mode, it's time to track how well you're doing it.

- Your Key Results from Chapter 5? Those are your lagging indicators; they measure whether you're hitting major milestones.
- Your X Factor? That's your leading indicator; the thing you need to do consistently to make progress.

The missing piece? Tracking those indicators to stay on course.

Tracking Leading and Lagging Indicators

Most people only track results—the lagging indicators—and wonder why they struggle to improve. The problem is that lagging indicators are measured after the fact. They tell you where you have arrived, but they don't help you navigate along the way.

That's where leading indicators come in. These are the behaviors that create the results.

Think of it this way:

- Lagging indicators track the destination. (Did I reach my Key Results?)
- Leading indicators track the journey. (Am I consistently taking the right actions?)

Let's bring this to life with a real example: my Flight Dashboard for writing this book.

Writing a Book: My Flight Dashboard

Objective: Publish "Be *Ooh La La*" by December 2025.

Lagging Indicators (Key Results)

- Complete Part I by January 2025 (~15,000 words).
- Complete Part II by March 2025 (~15,000 words).
- Complete Part III by May 2025 (~15,000 words).
- Edit, proofread, and format the layout by August 2025.
- Conduct pre-launch activities by October 2025.

These Key Results tell me where I need to be at different points. But if I only track these, I could fall behind without realizing it. Enter: leading indicators.

Leading Indicator (X Factor – Daily Action)

- Write 250 words per day. (If I miss a day, I make it up elsewhere.)
- Hit 7,500 words per month to stay on track for the monthly total.

By tracking my leading indicator (writing output) every day, I don't have to wait until the end of the month to know if I'm behind. If I start slipping, I can adjust immediately.

If I need additional support, I can introduce other key indicators to my dashboard, just like Sophie did in her business.

Sophie's Story: Expanding the Dashboard for Predictable Growth

Meet Sophie.

Sophie, a freelance design consultant specializing in brand and visual identity, wanted more than just a busy schedule, she wanted financial stability and peace of mind. For months, she felt like she was either drowning in client work or struggling to find new leads. Some months, she had plenty of business. Other months, she felt like she was waiting for something, anything, to happen.

Initially, she only tracked lagging indicators, including revenue and the number of new clients per month. But that didn't help her make progress in the moment. She had no way of knowing if she was taking enough action until it was too late.

So, she shifted her focus to leading indicators: the behaviors that drove results.

Her X Factor (Leading Indicator):

- Reach out to ten potential clients per week.

But she didn't stop there. She also added other key indicators to track her progress more holistically.

Her Flight Dashboard:

Leading Indicators:

- Ten outreach emails per week.
- Five networking calls per month.
- Three pieces of content per week to showcase her creative expertise and design thinking.

Lagging Indicators:

- Revenue growth.
- Number of new client contracts.
- Number of repeat clients.

By tracking both leading and lagging indicators, Sophie could see exactly what was working. If her outreach numbers were down, she could adjust before it affected her revenue. If her design content wasn't attracting leads, she could test different topics.

Within three months, her business had stabilized. She no longer felt like success was random.

She was in control.

Your Flight Dashboard – Build Your System

Just like a spacecraft has a dashboard to track speed, fuel, and trajectory, you need your system to track progress.

Here's how to set it up:
1. Define Your Lagging Indicators (Key Results)
What are the big-picture results you want to achieve? For example:

- Complete Part I of your book within three months.
- Gain 1,000 new subscribers in five months.
- Increase monthly revenue to $10,000 within two quarters.

2. Identify Your Leading Indicator (X Factor – Daily/Weekly Actions)
What's the one action that will drive the biggest impact? It might look like this:

- Write 250 words per day.
- Publish one YouTube video per week.
- Send ten outreach emails per week.

3. Add Supporting Indicators if Needed:

- Follow up with every client within forty-eight hours of their coaching session.
- Spend fifteen minutes per day engaging with your audience in comments or DMs.
- Reach out to one new collaborator or podcast host weekly.

4. Track & Adjust Weekly

- Check your leading indicators daily or weekly, depending on the nature of your goal
- Are you hitting them consistently?
- If not, adjust before it affects your lagging indicators.

There's a reason *Ooh La La* success feels so good; it's the result of intentional effort, tracked progress, and disciplined execution.

A goal without measurement is like a spacecraft with no navigation: you might get there, but you might not.

This is your mission. You're in control now. Your job is to stay aligned, stay aware, and course-correct when needed. But as you move forward, don't be surprised when something pushes back.

Momentum invites resistance. This is proof you have started.

Next, we'll look at the invisible forces that try to pull you off course, and how to overcome them with power and clarity.

4. THE MIGHTY RESISTANCE

"Resistance will tell you anything to keep you from doing your work. It will perjure, fabricate, falsify; it will seduce, bully, cajole. Resistance will assume any form to stop you from doing what you were born to do."
– Steven Pressfield, The War of Art

In Part I, we discussed fears, doubts, and limiting beliefs. That was the resistance of hesitation, the resistance before liftoff.

Now, you've launched, you've leaped, but if you thought Resistance stayed behind on the launchpad, think again.

It didn't wave goodbye. It climbed aboard, and it's not loud, instead, it's sneaks in through:

- The urge to take a break right when you were about to do something meaningful.
- The voice in your head whispers, "Maybe today isn't the best day to work on this."
- The shiny distraction that suddenly seems urgent (but isn't).

It's not just fear anymore, it is fatigue, rationalization, or comfort creeping back in.

Sometimes it calls itself perfectionism. Sometimes, fake productivity. But its goal is the same: stall your progress.

Here's what I've found: Resistance is part of the mission. If you're feeling it, it means you're doing something that matters.

Let's break down the everyday forms it can take—busyness, doubt, perfectionism, and fatigue—and learn how to spot them before they slow your momentum.

Because now that you're in motion, your greatest challenge is no longer about launching but staying in flight.

Let's keep going.

Resistance as "Busyness"

When you're working toward something meaningful, resistance won't stop you directly, it will redirect you.

Ever notice that just as you sit down to work, you suddenly remember:

- You should check your inbox, just in case.
- You should tweak that presentation, it could be better.
- You should clean your desk; you'll be more productive that way.

It's not procrastination, exactly. You feel productive, but you're not making real progress.

One of resistance's best tricks is keeping you busy with things that feel productive but don't move the needle.

Trust me, I know this one well. During my book planning phase, I'd often fill my time with reorganizing notes, reviewing outlines (again), or diving into research rabbit holes. It felt like progress. But deep down, I knew I was avoiding the real work: writing.

Busyness can look responsible on the outside, but sometimes, it's resistance dressed in a very convincing disguise.

Resistance as Doubt Creeping Back In

You already decided to go for it. You committed. But resistance still lurks, waiting for the right moment to plant seeds of doubt.

- "Is this even working?"
- "Am I making enough progress?"
- "What if this isn't the right path?"

Resistance doesn't have to convince you to quit. It just has to make you question whether you should slow down.

If you start second-guessing yourself, momentum weakens.

I've been there. Even after committing to this book and feeling fired up about the mission, there were moments I wondered, "Is this landing? Will anyone care about this framework? Should I pivot halfway through?"

The truth is, those questions aren't signs that you're failing, they're signs that you're doing something that matters.

Resistance as Perfectionism – The Never-Ending Edit Loop

This one is my passionate battle with resistance.

When I'm writing, I constantly feel the pull to go back and rework what I've already written. Just a quick fix here. A minor adjustment there.

The problem? That's resistance in disguise.

I tell myself, *I'll catch up on the writing over the weekend.* But I know how that story goes.

There's a saying in the book world: "Just write the Shitty First Draft (SFD)." It's not elegant, but it works. The entire focus should be on completing the first draft of the full manuscript before considering editing.

But it's hard. Really hard.

- I'll convince myself that the opening of a chapter could be sharper.
- I'll rework a paragraph instead of adding new words.
- I'll tinker with sentence structure instead of hitting my daily word target.

Resistance loves perfectionism because it feels productive, but it slows everything down.

The only way through? Keep writing. Keep going. Keep stacking words, even when I want to stop.

Resistance as the "Take the Day Off" Trap

This one is sneaky.

If I've had a long day, resistance gets smarter. Instead of stopping me outright, it offers me a "reasonable" excuse.

- "Take the day off, Raphael. You've earned it."
- "Not today. Just write tomorrow."
- "You won't write anything good if your brain is tired. Better to wait."

Sounds logical, right? I mean, I should be in the right mindset to write, shouldn't I?

Here's my Ooh La La tip: Push through. Momentum will meet you there.

Some of the best ideas come right when I am about to give up.

Every time I ignore the excuse and start writing, even if it's only for five minutes, something clicks. Words flow. The resistance weakens.

Action wins every time.

Why Resistance is Proof You're on the Right Path

Here's something to remember: Resistance shows up most when you're onto something big.

You don't feel resistance when you're doing things that don't matter.

- No one feels resistance to watching TV.
- No one feels resistance when scrolling through social media.
- No one feels resistance to taking the easy path.

Resistance is a sign that you're doing something meaningful.

The stronger the resistance, the bigger the impact of what you're working toward.

So, the next time resistance shows up, don't see it as an obstacle. See it as confirmation that you're on the right path.

How to Beat Resistance and Keep Moving Toward *Ooh La La*

Since resistance is always lurking, you need strategies to manage it effectively.

Here's how:

1. Expect Resistance Daily – Be Ready for It
   Astronauts don't panic when turbulence hits; they've trained for it. Resistance is your turbulence. Expect it, prep for it, and stay steady. The same goes for resistance.
    - Expect distractions to pop up.
    - Expect doubt to sneak in.
    - Expect moments of fatigue where you don't feel like doing the work.

   When you anticipate resistance, you prepare for it.
2. Stick to Your Leading Indicators (Stay Focused on Action)
   Remember our Flight Dashboard from earlier? This is why tracking your leading indicators is critical.
   When resistance shows up, you don't have to rely on willpower. You rely on your system.
    - Doubt creeping in? Stick to your daily non-negotiable, it's your anchor.
    - Feel like skipping a work session? Just do the minimum and keep the habit alive.
    - Feel overwhelmed? Go back to small, simple actions.

Resistance hates consistency. Stick to the plan, and resistance weakens.

3. Shut Down Resistance Fast (Before It Gains Power)
   The longer you let resistance sit, the stronger it gets.
   That's why you must act before it has a chance to take hold.
   - If you feel the urge to delay, start immediately.
   - If you catch yourself overthinking, act before reasoning with yourself.
   - If perfectionism creeps in, set a deadline and hit "publish."
   - Don't give resistance time to negotiate with you. Move first.

Resistance is the Price of Progress

Resistance doesn't go away. It's part of the mission.
The only question is: *Will you persevere, or will it hold you back?*

- Every time you choose action over resistance, you get stronger.
- Every time you push through self-doubt, you get closer to *Ooh La La*.
- Every time you refuse to slow down, you leave resistance behind.

And when you hit the next level? Resistance resets. But now, you've got the playbook.

Now that you know resistance is part of the ride, where exactly are you in your mission?

Next, we'll map out your journey using the S-Curve, as each phase of growth presents different challenges and strategies.

Let's find out where you are and how to keep accelerating forward.

OOH LA LA HIGHLIGHTS

STEP 8: LIFTOFF, YOU ARE IN THE DRIVER'S SEAT

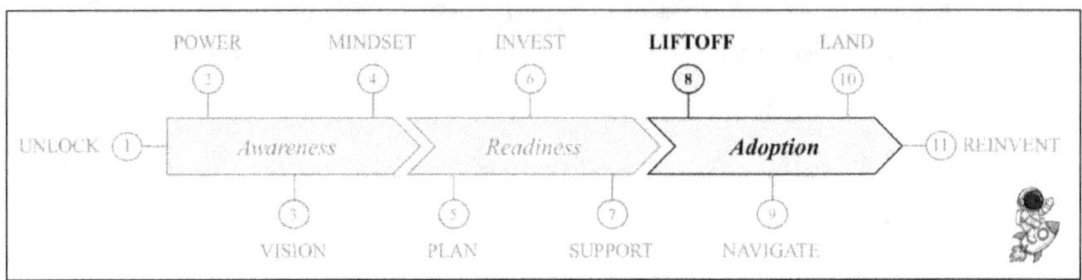

MISSION BRIEF

Action is the true catalyst for success. Success begins the moment action replaces hesitation. Momentum is built through movement, not waiting for perfect conditions. Progress occurs by taking consistent steps forward, trusting the process, and adjusting along the way.

CRITICAL SYSTEMS CHECK

- Action Over Perfection – The perfect time will never come. The only way forward is to take the first step.
- The Momentum Effect – Small, consistent actions compound into significant results.
- Navigational Laws for Success: Understanding the forces that shape progress.
  - The Law of Vibration – Your mindset determines what you attract.
  - The Law of Action – Success comes from taking consistent, aligned action toward your goals.
  - The Law of Compensation – Value creation leads to greater rewards.
  - The Law of Authenticity – The more you embrace your true self, the more doors open.
- Overcoming Resistance – The journey won't be smooth: doubt, sneaky distractions, and setbacks will arise. Success belongs to those who push through, stay consistent, and keep moving despite resistance.

PILOT'S REFLECTION

1. Am I acting in alignment with who I truly am, or just doing what I think I "should" do?
2. What consistent action, no matter how small, can I take today that builds momentum toward my vision?
3. What internal resistance is currently slowing me down, and how can I move through it with intention?

NEXT COORDINATES

We'll look at the natural rhythms behind every big journey. Growth doesn't move in a straight line; it rises, steadies, and eventually shifts. Knowing how to navigate these phases is what keeps you moving forward instead of stalling out.

CHAPTER 9

•

NAVIGATE THE JOURNEY

1. UNDERSTANDING THE S-CURVE

Every bold mission, whether launching a business, creating a body of artwork, writing a book, designing a new product, switching careers, or reshaping your life… follows a unique trajectory. It rarely unfolds in a straight line, nor does it offer instant success. Instead, progress follows a distinct pattern, a curve that rises, stabilizes, and eventually demands reinvention.

This pattern, known as the S-Curve, also referred to as the Sigmoid Curve or the Success Curve, provides a roadmap for understanding your current position, anticipating the challenges ahead, and navigating them effectively.

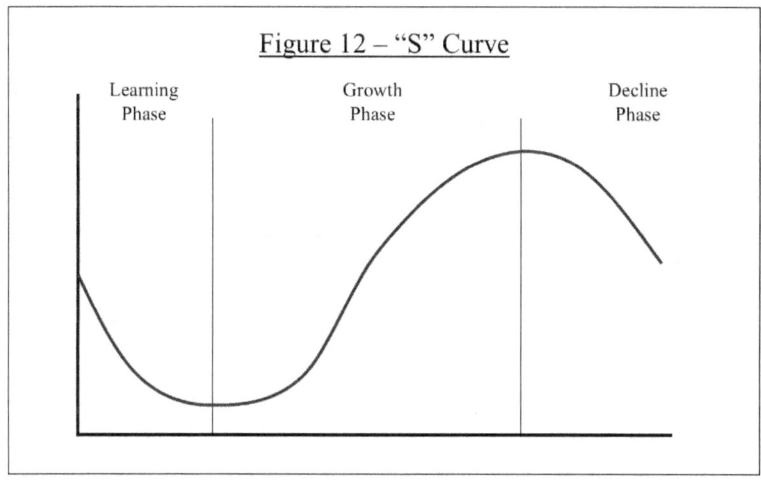

Figure 12 – "S" Curve

The Learning Phase – Early Wins and First Challenges

The beginning of any journey is exciting. Energy is high, motivation fuels action, and early wins come quickly. You spot signs of progress, small but promising, and they reinforce the belief that you're on the right path. It feels easier than expected, and your confidence builds.

But eventually, things shift. The momentum slows. What once felt effortless now demands consistent, focused effort. Progress becomes uneven.

Obstacles appear. Doubt creeps in. Many mistake this dip for failure when it's simply the second half of the learning curve, the stretch where persistence gets tested. This is where most people give up, unaware they're just steps away from true momentum. But those who keep going learn that struggle is a signpost pointing to growth, not a stop sign.

The Growth Phase – Momentum and Mastery

Once past the turbulence of the Learning Phase, something shifts. Systems fall into place, skills sharpen, and your effort begins to translate into tangible results. Instead of pushing uphill, you start to feel a pull forward. What once required full effort now happens with greater efficiency.

This is the phase where success compounds. Your processes are working, your confidence is solid, and the results start reflecting your effort. However, it is not automatic, it still requires sustaining focus, refining strategies, and resisting complacency. Those who maintain discipline in this phase set themselves up for long-term success. But those who assume momentum will last without intentional effort may unknowingly drift toward stagnation.

The Decline Phase – Stagnation or Reinvention

Eventually, what once worked starts losing its edge. The methods that once drove success no longer deliver the same results. If left unaddressed, this leads to stagnation. Some people ignore the signs, holding on to past achievements while their progress plateaus or, even worse, declines. Others recognize the shift and take action.

This is the critical choice. Reinvent or decline. The people who thrive over the long term are the ones who anticipate the need for change and act before the curve bottoms out. Reinvention is the key to staying relevant and avoiding a slow fade.

Each phase presents its challenges, and failing to recognize where you are can lead to missteps. Early on, success can feel misleadingly easy. Before growth takes off, doubt can convince you to quit too soon. Along the growth journey, failing to evolve can lead to decline.

Your ability to recognize your position on the curve determines your next move.

From Phases to Pitfalls – The Hidden Traps Along the Curve

Now, understanding the S-Curve is powerful, but it's only part of the story. Each phase along the curve presents hidden traps. These aren't always obvious. They often disguise themselves as success, comfort, or routine. That's what makes them so dangerous.

If you're not paying attention, these traps can slow you down, knock you off course, or even convince you to quit.

The good news? Once you know what to look for, you can avoid them.

Let's start at the very beginning, right after launch, where everything feels almost too easy…

2. THE HONEYMOON TRAP

I Didn't See It Coming!

When I first sat down to write this book, I was on fire.

I had everything ready: my outline was solid, my stories were prepped, my playlist was queued, and my coffee was strong. I carved out a quiet weekend and dove in. By the end of that first writing session, I had cranked out 1,800 words like it was nothing. The ideas felt sharp, the rhythm was smooth, and I thought to myself, "This is going to be easier than I thought."

I closed my laptop feeling proud, and I figured I had earned a few days off. After all, if I could knock out nearly 2,000 words in one sitting, I could easily pick it back up later.

But then a week went by.

And I hadn't written a single word.

That's when I realized I had fallen into a trap. A subtle, sneaky one. One that catches more people than you'd think.

It's called The Honeymoon Trap.

What Is The Honeymoon Trap?

Picture this: you've just launched your creative or professional mission, and the early momentum is thrilling.

- You land your first freelance client after sending a single cold email.
- You sit down to write the first chapter of your novel, and it

practically writes itself.

- You commit to a new fitness plan, and the first few weeks feel incredible.
- You upload your first video, and your YouTube channel gains early traction.
- You open your sketchbook, and the ideas just keep flowing.

Everything feels light, fun, and effortless. You feel like the possibilities are without limits.

It's as if you've broken through the atmosphere and are now floating in space; weightless, frictionless, untouchable.

This is the Honeymoon Phase: the exhilarating beginning of a journey where things seem to work better than expected, and the world feels full of possibility.

But there's something most people don't realize: That high doesn't last.

If you're not prepared, the drop that follows can feel like failure.

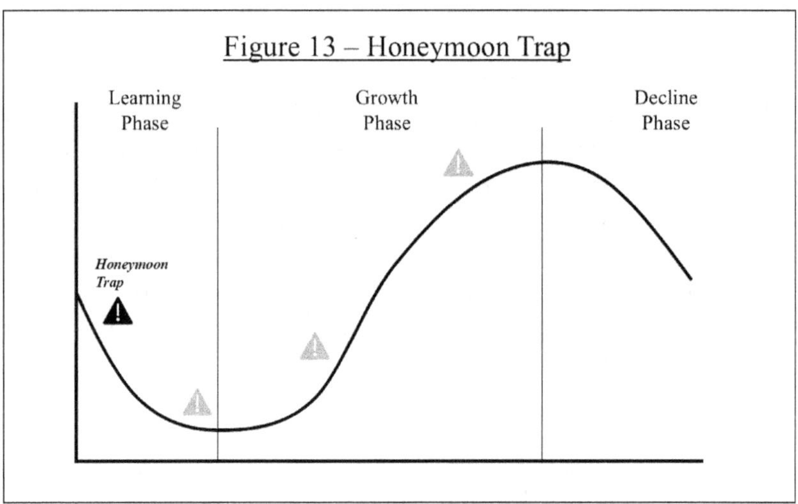

Why Is This a Trap?

When your early efforts lead to success with minimal friction, it becomes easy, almost automatic, to assume that things will continue this way.

- You believe the clients will continue to show up effortlessly.
- You expect your writing to always flow with ease.
- You assume your motivation will never dip.

- You count on the ideas to arrive right on time, every time.

But eventually, resistance returns.
That second client is harder to land.
The writing stalls.
The creative energy wavers.
The new habit starts to feel like actual work.
And when this happens, many people start to panic.
"May*be I'm not as good at this as I thought.*"
"Was that early success just luck?"
*"Why does everythin*g suddenly feel harder?"
Here's what you need to know: this is not a sign that something's wrong. It's a sign that you've exited the Honeymoon Phase and entered the real work of the journey. It means the spark that got you started did its job. Now, it's time to build the structure that will carry you forward.

How to Avoid The Honeymoon Trap

If you find yourself in the Honeymoon Phase right now, first, pause and celebrate. Starting something new takes courage. You've already crossed a line most people never do.

Now comes the more important part: making sure you *keep going.*

Here's how to do that.

1. Build Systems Before the Motivation Wears Off

Right now, things feel exciting. The work flows easily. Your energy is high.

That's precisely why this is the best possible moment to create systems, so that when the excitement fades (and it will), your momentum doesn't. Because motivation is temporary, but systems endure.

- If you're writing a book, commit to a daily word count now. Treat it like an appointment, not a mood. As author Somerset Maugham once said, *"I only write when inspiration strikes. Fortunately, it strikes every morning at nine o'clock."*

- If you're building a business, pay close attention to what's already working. Turn those actions into repeatable processes. In the words of Dwayne "The Rock" Johnson, *"Success isn't always about greatness. It's about consistency."*

- If you're creating a portfolio, carve out protected time to make things. Don't wait for inspiration. Artist Chuck Close put it best: *"Inspiration is for amateurs. The rest of us just show up and get to work."*

The lesson is simple: momentum comes from consistent, focused movement, not magic.

2. Identify What's Working and Do More of It

Your early success wasn't an accident. Something you did worked. Your job now is to find it, name it, and double down.

- If a particular topic resonates with your audience, turn it into a series.
- If your best ideas come late at night, stop fighting it and protect that time.
- If client calls go better when you lead with a story, make storytelling part of your playbook.
- If your creative energy spikes after a morning walk, structure your day to support that rhythm.

You don't need to reinvent everything; you need to pay attention to the signals and steer intentionally.

3. Expect the Dip Because It's Coming

There will come a day when you don't feel like doing the work.

There will be a stretch where progress feels slow, or even invisible.

You will question your process. You may even question yourself.

That's not failure. It's the next level of the climb.

If you expect the dip, you won't be blindsided by it. You'll be ready.

Write this somewhere you'll see it often:

"What's one thing I'll keep doing, even when I don't feel like it?"

That becomes your anchor.

That becomes your non-negotiable.

That's what will carry you when motivation disappears.

The *Ooh La La* Scale – Navigating the Honeymoon Phase

Wondering how well you're handling this stage? Use the *Ooh La La* Scale to check in:

Level	Mindset	Action	Outcome
Ooh (Trapped)	"This is easy! I don't need a plan."	Coasting. Assuming momentum will last forever.	Crashes when resistance shows up.

Ooh La (Drifting)	"I know the dip is coming… but I'll deal with it later."	Inconsistent. Relies on motivation.	Progress slows. Doubt creeps in.
Ooh La La (Focused)	"I'm using this momentum to build strong habits."	Establishes systems. Tracks key actions.	Maintains steady progress. Ready for the next phase.

Where do you fall right now?

If you're in *Ooh*, it's time to get grounded. The trap is real. Build habits before momentum slips.

If you're in *Ooh La*, you're close. Start turning what's working into systems you can trust.

If you're in *Ooh La La*, stay consistent. You're setting the stage for long-term success.

Back to My Story

Remember that 1,800-word writing weekend, the one that made me feel unstoppable?

Well, it barely resembles what made it into the final version of this book.

Turns out, early drafts are just that, drafts. The real magic came later, when I built a system.

Here's what that looked like:

- On weekdays, I focused on writing key sections, even if they were messy.
- On weekends, I took time to review, connect ideas, and refine what I had written.

That rhythm gave me momentum when I didn't feel inspired and space to polish when I did. It helped me keep going through both the highs and the lows.

That system is why this book exists.

So, if you're riding the Honeymoon high right now, enjoy it. Use it. But don't rely on it.

The spark is what gets you going, the structure is what makes it real.

Practical Exercise – Lock in Your Strategy

Step 1: Identify What's Working

- What early wins have you had so far?
- What specific actions led to those wins?

Step 2: Systematize It

- How can you turn those actions into habits?
- What is one daily or weekly commitment you can make?

Step 3: Plan for the Dip

- What is the one thing you'll keep doing, even when motivation fades?
- Who can help hold you accountable when the initial excitement wears off?

Right now, you're floating in zero gravity. Energy is high, and progress feels smooth.

But weightlessness won't last forever.

Because of the next trap? That's where trouble gets real.

3. HOUSTON, WE HAVE A PROBLEM

Leo, a talented piano performer, was ready to quit.

He had just wrapped his latest run of shows, and the energy was off. The crowd was small. The venue had made last-minute changes to the lighting, throwing off the atmosphere he had carefully designed. Ticket sales had come in at half the number he had projected.

Afterward, he sat alone in his car, staring at the steering wheel and replaying the entire night in his mind.

"Maybe I'm not cut out for this."

"Maybe people don't want what I'm offering anymore."

"Maybe I should pivot now before I waste any more time."

He wasn't just tired. He was disoriented, discouraged. Worst of all, this wave of doubt came after what had felt like incredible momentum.

Not too long ago, his early shows had sold out. The crowds were electric. Even the press had taken notice. For a while, it seemed as if everything was lining up perfectly.

But now?

That momentum had slowed and so had his belief in himself.

What Leo didn't realize in that moment was something essential: He was just three feet from gold.

The Three Feet from Gold Trap – Why People Quit Too Soon

The phrase "three feet from gold" comes from a story in Think and Grow Rich by Napoleon Hill.

In the story, a prospector spends months digging in pursuit of gold. After endless effort and no visible results, he gives up. He sells the land to someone else. The new owner brings in a mining expert, who surveys the land and digs just a few feet further, striking one of the richest gold veins ever discovered.

Just three feet.

That's how close he was to everything he had worked for.

This is exactly where many of us find ourselves right before the breakthrough. It can be very frustrating and daunting; I like to call this place the "Pit of Despair."

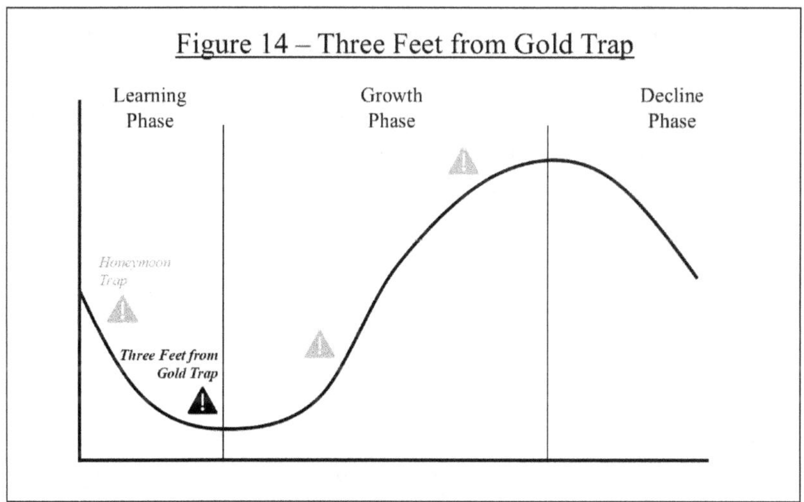

Figure 14 – Three Feet from Gold Trap

This Is the Pit of Despair

In contrast to the Honeymoon Phase Trap, the Pit of Despair hits after you've already covered some ground. The initial excitement has faded, and you're facing the slower, tougher grind. The results don't seem to match your effort, and the momentum you once had feels like it's slipping away.

And then the questions start.

"Is this even working?"

"Should I be doing something else?"

"Am I wasting my time?"

This is not burnout. And it is not failure. This is the stretch of the Learning Phase that feels heavy, discouraging, and confusing. What you do here matters more than you realize.

Because this is the moment that separates those who finish from those who quit.

Mistaking Resistance for Failure

This is where many people walk away, not because they're not good enough but because they've misread the moment.

- The entrepreneur who has worked for months without consistent revenue decides to scrap the idea entirely and move on to something new.
- The filmmaker who runs into post-production roadblocks considers shelving the entire project.
- The artist whose online growth has plateaued suddenly stops creating.
- The athlete who's been training for weeks without visible results begins to question whether they're even built for this.

They reach the Pit and assume the struggle is a sign to stop.

But it's not.

Resistance is not failure. It's feedback.

The Pit is not the end of the journey; it's part of the journey.

And if you need a reminder of what's possible when you respond with adaptation instead of retreat, look to Apollo 13.

Apollo 13 – Reframing the Mission to Save It

In 1970, NASA launched the Apollo 13 mission with a singular goal: to land on the moon.

But halfway through the journey, disaster struck. An oxygen tank exploded, tearing through the spacecraft, crippling its power supply, and flooding it with carbon dioxide. In a single moment, the dream of a moon landing was gone. The new mission was survival.

Suddenly, three astronauts were trapped in a damaged spacecraft nearly 200,000 miles from Earth. Oxygen was running low. Heat was vanishing. Communications flickered. Every system they had trained to rely on was compromised. Families gathered in front of TVs, the world watched in silence, and no one knew if the crew would ever make it back alive.

The emotional toll was immense. The astronauts battled fear, exhaustion, and the weight of knowing one wrong calculation could mean death. In Houston, engineers faced their own pressure cooker: the knowledge that millions of people were watching them try to solve problems that no one had prepared for. The stakes could not have been higher.

Yet, instead of giving in to panic, they reframed the crisis. The crew and ground team asked:

"What can we do with what we've got?"

They tore up old procedures and improvised new ones. Using duct tape, cardboard, and spare parts, they fashioned a CO_2 filter. They rationed power down to the last volt, rewriting the re-entry plan by hand. Every move carried risk, but they chose action over despair.

Against all odds, Apollo 13 made it home safely. What was once a failed mission became a triumph of ingenuity, resilience, and reframing under pressure.

The plan failed. But the people didn't.

Reframing the Pit – The Obstacle Is the Way

In *The Obstacle Is the Way*, Ryan Holiday puts it simply:

"Obstacles aren't the enemy; they are the path forward."

When you're deep in the Pit, you have two choices:

1. See the challenge as proof that things are not working and give up.
2. Reframe the challenge as an opportunity to grow, adapt, and move forward with clarity.

The Apollo 13 team didn't waste energy wishing things had gone differently. They focused on what they could control:

- *"What can we do with what we have?"*
- *"What is the next right move?"*
- *"How can we turn this problem into our advantage?"*

You can do the same.

Back to Leo – Three Feet from Gold

After that difficult night, Leo was on the edge of giving up. He had poured his savings, time, and pride into building his performance career, yet the returns weren't lining up. Empty chairs stared back at him, canceled venues felt like rejection letters, and silence from the media cut deeper than criticism.

The stakes were real. If he quit, it wouldn't just mean shelving a project; it would mean admitting to himself, his family, and his community that the dream he had sacrificed so much for wasn't going to make it. On the other hand, if he pushed forward without change, he risked burning out completely. He was standing in his own Pit of Despair, staring at two paths that both felt heavy.

That's when he reframed the questions:

- What if slow ticket sales were simply feedback, not failure?
- What if venue cancellations meant he needed to expand his options?
- What if the lack of media coverage was a signal to build his own platform?

Leo realized that his current approach wasn't enough. He didn't need a new dream; he needed a new strategy. So, he adjusted the flight plan.

Turning Reframes into Results

Leo changed the way he thought and the way he worked.

1. Focus on Process Over Outcome

Rather than obsessing over empty seats, Leo focused on actions within his control:

- He committed to reaching out to five new venues each week.
- He began posting one short performance video every day.
- He proactively pitched five new journalists every month.

His mindset shifted from "waiting for results" to "showing up consistently."

Ooh La La Lesson: Progress is a byproduct of rhythm, not hope. Results follow action.

2. Lower Expectations—But Not Standards

Leo had assumed that because his first shows were successful, every event would need to be a hit.

But after researching other successful performers, he discovered a more grounded truth: not every event would be a home run, and that was okay.

He shifted his mindset from "every show must succeed" to "every show is a rep that builds the bigger picture."

Ooh La La Lesson: A setback doesn't mean failure. It means you're still training.

3. Cut Off the Escape Route

Leo found himself tempted to pivot: *"Maybe I should just focus on weddings, maybe I should compose instead of perform."*

Instead of acting on that impulse, he made a personal commitment: six more months, no matter what. No distractions. No bailouts.

Ooh La La Lesson: Growth needs roots. Don't abandon the mission before it has time to flourish.

4. Lean on Your Ground Crew

Leo reached out to a mentor who had successfully built a similar performance business.

The mentor listened, then offered a piece of advice that shifted everything:

"It always feels slow before it clicks. It takes longer than you want but not as long as you fear."

That perspective helped Leo re-center. He wasn't failing. He was simply in the Pit, and now, he had a map.

Ooh La La Lesson: You don't have to navigate the hard parts alone. The right support can help you stay in the game.

The *Ooh La La* Scale – Three Feet from Gold

Not sure where you stand right now? Use this as a check-in:

Level	Mindset	Action	Outcome
Ooh	"This isn't working. Maybe I should quit."	Pulls back. Look for exits.	Stops just before the breakthrough.
Ooh La	"This is harder than I thought."	Inconsistent action. Doubt clouds progress.	Some momentum but fragile foundation.
Ooh La La	"This challenge is feedback, not failure. How can I reframe it?"	Strategic adaptation. Focus on controllables.	Momentum builds. The obstacle becomes the breakthrough opening.

Where are you right now?

- If you are in *Ooh*, don't walk away. You may be closer than you think.

- If you are in *Ooh La*, reframe struggle as training and adapt your systems.
- If you are in *Ooh La La*, you've learned to reframe obstacles into opportunities. You are not just surviving the Pit; you're using it to rise.

Three Feet from Gold—For Real

Three months after nearly giving up, Leo's momentum returned.

- One of his performance clips went viral.
- A local influencer attended a show and posted about the experience.
- New venues began reaching out to him directly.

His following three shows sold out.

He had been three feet from gold, but he kept digging, and the gold revealed itself.

Before You Quit, Pause

If you find yourself in a slow season…

If you're questioning everything…

If you're wondering whether to keep going…

Pause.

Take a breath.

You're not failing. You may simply be in the Pit, closer than you realize to everything you've been working toward.

So, dig again.

The Growth Phase, the next stretch of your mission, is where the real magic happens. But you will only reach it if you stay in the game, learn from the friction, and commit to leveling up.

4. MASTERING THE JOURNEY

Meet Emma, an HR consulting business owner. Emma sat at her desk, surrounded by color-coded project boards, unread emails, and back-to-back meetings that left her little time to breathe. Her HR consulting business was thriving, clients were happy, results were strong, and revenue was steady.

But she was drowning.

Every decision ran through her. Every deliverable depended on her. Every hour of progress came at the cost of her energy and time.

That's when it hit her.

She wasn't running a business; she was trapped inside one.

Despite all her success, she had created something that couldn't function without her. The systems, the team, even the growth itself—they all depended on her personal involvement. If she stepped away, the whole machine would grind to a halt.

Emma had made it through the Honeymoon Phase. She had climbed out of the Pit of Despair. But now, she was in new territory, one that requires an entirely different mindset:

The Growth Phase.

This is where many people get stuck because they fail to adapt their approach as their mission evolves.

Welcome to the Growth Phase

You've navigated the hard parts. You launched your mission, survived the setbacks, and refused to quit when things got tough.

Now, for the first time, something powerful is unfolding.

You are experiencing real growth.

Your actions are compounding. The systems you put in place are starting to generate results. The opportunities that once seemed distant now feel within reach.

But there is a new challenge ahead. The Growth Phase requires you to build the right foundation to sustain and not stifle that growth.

If you're not careful, you can unknowingly step into the most deceptive trap of all: the Founder's Trap.

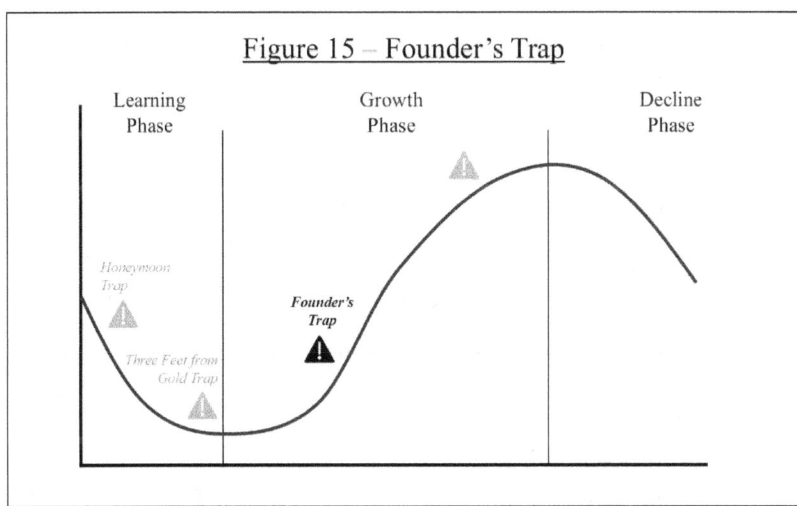

Figure 15 – Founder's Trap

The Founder's Trap – Why Growth Stalls

In the early stages, you were the one doing everything. You created the product, closed the deals, answered the emails, and wore every hat in the building. That was necessary back then.

But now? It is holding you back.

The Founder's Trap happens when the person who launched the mission can't or won't release control, becoming the bottleneck without even noticing.

- The entrepreneur who insists on managing every task because "no one else can do it like I can."
- The leader who hires help but micromanages every detail.
- The creative who clings to every part of the process out of fear that letting go will lower the quality.

What they don't see is that the real risk is stalling their growth. When your mission depends solely on your energy, attention, or time, you will eventually reach a ceiling.

Scaling requires a different mindset. It demands that you stop being the doer and step fully into the role of the leader.

What Changes in the Growth Phase?

The mission has officially shifted. You are no longer fighting for liftoff. You are now in orbit.

In this phase:

1. You're operating with consistency. The systems you built are creating reliable momentum.
2. You're no longer reacting to every crisis. You have room to think strategically.
3. You're starting to see real leverage with bigger clients, wider reach, and greater opportunities. But to seize that potential, you have to grow beyond yourself. If you keep operating the same way you did at launch, burnout will set in, and your mission will stall.

Emma's Shift – From Technician to CEO

Emma had already built something strong. Her HR consultancy was making $150,000 per year, and her reputation in the industry was stellar.

But her business could not grow beyond her.

She had a few contractors and freelancers, but she was still involved in every major decision. She was still overseeing every project. She was still the bottleneck.

To change that, Emma had to make three key shifts:

1. She stopped inserting herself into every project and instead built a management team she could trust.
2. She hired specialists, not just assistants, people who could take full ownership of key areas.
3. She stepped out of daily execution and into long-term strategy, focusing on leadership and growth.

Over the course of five years, her business grew from $150,000 to $4 million per year. She built a team of more than twenty employees. She was no longer stuck in the trenches. She was leading from the front.

That shift from doing to leading was the difference between a profitable business and a scalable one.

How to Lead Through the Growth Phase

1. Fine-Tune Your Processes

Now that momentum is on your side, it is time to optimize.

- Automate tasks that repeat themselves. If it happens more than once, create a system.
- Delegate responsibilities that others can handle 80 percent as well as you can.
- Refine your workflows to remove friction, delays, or duplication.

Growth without efficiency eventually collapses under its own weight. The more streamlined your systems, the further and faster you can scale.

2. Suit Up for Growth – The Space Suit Strategy

Think of your daily tasks like different kinds of gear. Some fit you perfectly. Some drag you down. To lead your mission at a high level, you need to spend most of your time in the gear designed for you.

Here is how to break it down:

- Slippers – Comfortable but completely unfit for space. These are low-skill, low-impact tasks that distract from your real mission. Eliminate or delegate them immediately.
- Standard Suit – Functional, generic work. You can do it, but it doesn't energize or elevate you. These are strong candidates for automation or outsourcing.
- Second-Hand Suit – Tasks you were once good at and maybe even proud of, but they no longer require your direct involvement.

They don't fit you anymore, even if they once did. Pass them off to someone else who can wear them better now.

- Space Suit – High-impact, high-leverage work that only you can do. This is your zone of leadership, strategy, and growth. When you're in your Space Suit, you are doing the work that moves the entire mission forward.

The biggest mistake leaders make is staying too long in the Second-Hand Suit: doing work they've outgrown instead of stepping fully into their highest role.

Emma was excellent at client work, but that was not her Space Suit. Her real value lay in leading the team, setting the vision, and building the infrastructure. Once she stepped into that role, everything accelerated.

Practical Exercise: Suit Up with Intention

1. List Your Daily Tasks
   Write down everything you do in a typical week.
2. Categorize Each Task
   Label each one as Slippers, Standard Gear, Second-Hand Suit, or Space Suit.
3. Offload What Doesn't Fit
   Identify what can be delegated, automated, or removed entirely.
4. Prioritize Your Space Suit Work
   Block time for your highest-impact work. Protect it fiercely. That is where your leadership lives.

3. Plan for Sustainable Growth

Rapid growth is exciting, but it can be dangerous if you're not structurally prepared.

Ask yourself:

- Can your systems handle a sudden increase in demand?
- Do you have the necessary personnel in place to maintain quality as you scale up?
- Are your finances strong enough to support expansion without overextending?

Without a solid foundation, growth can create more stress than success.

Build before you need it. Then, when opportunity knocks, you will be ready to open the door.

Avoiding the Founder's Trap – The *Ooh La La* Scale

Level	Mindset	Action	Outcome
Ooh	"I have to do everything myself."	Continues to do everything alone.	Growth hits a ceiling.
Ooh La	"I have help, but I still control everything."	Hesitant to let go. Micromanages.	Progress is slow and inefficient.
Ooh La La	"I'm leading, not just doing."	Delegating. Optimizing. Scaling.	Growth accelerates and sustains.

Where do you see yourself right now?

- If you are in *Ooh*, it is time to release control and trust others.
- If you are in *Ooh La*, your next step is to lead, not manage, ditch that Second-Hand Suit.
- If you are in *Ooh La La*, reinforce your systems and keep scaling with intention.

Are You Leading Your Mission—Or Just Running It?

The Growth Phase requires you to zoom out.

It's no longer just about proving the idea works. It's about building something that can thrive without your involvement in every decision.

The key question becomes: Are you acting as a technician, a manager, or a CEO?

So far, you have navigated the Learning Phase, weathering turbulence, surviving resistance, and establishing systems. You stepped into the Growth Phase, where momentum builds, leadership matters, and the mission expands beyond you. You've reached the top of the Growth Phase, the peak of the curve, approaching your destination.

Are there still traps to be mindful of? Absolutely. One of the most dangerous waits on the far side of achievement, but we'll circle back to that in Chapter 11.

Before we charge ahead, it is time to pause and reflect.

Where are you in the journey? Are you finally arriving at your destination?

The next skill to master isn't speed but precision.

Next: Sticking the Landing

In Chapter 10, we will shift our focus to the art of Sticking the Landing, learning to recognize when you have arrived, honoring the distance you have traveled, and creating space to experience success fully.

It's easy to stay in a constant state of pursuit, always chasing the next milestone. But if you never stop to acknowledge what you've built, you risk missing the very reward you were working toward.

Now is the time to pause, recalibrate, and take in the view.

The mission isn't over yet, but how you land matters just as much as how you launch.

OOH *LA LA* HIGHLIGHTS

STEP 9: NAVIGATE THE JOURNEY

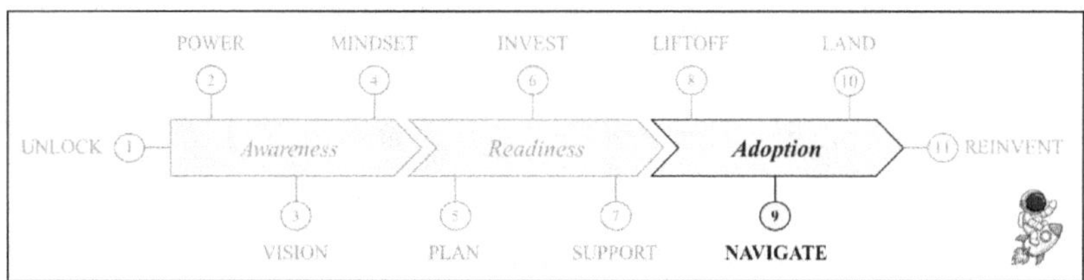

MISSION BRIEF

Progress is never a straight line; it follows an S-Curve of learning, growth, and eventual reinvention. The early phases of success come with predictable traps that can stall momentum if not recognized. Understanding where you are on the curve ensures you push forward rather than get stuck or give up too soon.

CRITICAL SYSTEMS CHECK

- The first three traps along the learning and growth phases:
- The Honeymoon Trap – The Illusion of Early Success
  - The Danger – Initial wins can feel effortless, leading to overconfidence and a false sense of sustainability.
  - The Solution – Build systems early. Momentum won't last without structure, discipline, and consistency.
- The Three Feet from Gold Trap – Quitting Right Before the Breakthrough
  - The Danger – Progress slows, obstacles arise, and doubt creeps in, causing many to abandon their efforts too soon.
  - The Solution – Reframe struggles as part of the process. Push through the resistance, and you'll often find success just on the other side.
- The Founder's Trap – Becoming Your Bottleneck
  - The Danger – Growth stalls when one person tries to do everything. Micromanaging or refusing to delegate limits scale and success.

- The Solution – Shift from doing to leading. Optimize, delegate, and expand beyond yourself to sustain long-term momentum.

PILOT'S REFLECTION

1. Which of the first phases of the S-Curve are you in: Learning? Growth?
2. Have you mistaken temporary difficulty for failure?
3. Are you holding onto control in ways that limit your success?

NEXT COORDINATES:

You've piloted through turbulence; now it's time to recognize when you've arrived. Sticking the landing is its discipline, and it begins with understanding what success truly looks like.

CHAPTER 10

•

LAND WITH INTENTION

1. HARVEST WHAT YOU SOW

You've given everything to this journey: your time, energy, your late nights, and quiet sacrifices. You've faced doubt, pushed through fear, and kept going when it would've been easier to turn back. And now, here you are. Right at the edge of everything you worked for.

This is the moment before the moment. The one where your hands might shake, not from uncertainty but from the quiet, powerful realization: You made it.

After all the effort, something has changed.

At first, it's just a shimmer in the distance, barely distinguishable from the vast unknown. Then, as you draw closer, the shape sharpens. The place you've been aiming for, the destination you set out toward when this mission began, finally comes into view.

The planet isn't theoretical anymore. It's not just coordinates on a map or a dream scribbled in a notebook. It's real. It's right in front of you.

For so long, you've been in motion. One step, then another. Navigating turbulence, recalibrating course, staying focused on what's next. But now, the landscape of your goal is fully visible beneath you.

And yet, despite this undeniable moment of arrival, something strange happens to so many people at this stage.

They don't land.

The Marathon Runner Who Didn't Stop

Imagine this: a runner trains for over a year.

They wake up before dawn, lace up their shoes in the dark, and log mile after mile in every kind of weather. Their life begins to orbit around the race: every meal, every rest day, every decision shaped by the goal of crossing the finish line.

Finally, race day arrives. The adrenaline is high, the crowd is buzzing, and the course stretches out in front of them. They push through fatigue, ignore the voice in their head telling them to quit, and after twenty-six grueling miles… they do it.

They cross the finish line.

And then?

They just keep running. No pause. No breath. No joy.

They don't smile. Don't raise their arms in triumph. Don't even look up.

They check their watch, give a subtle nod, and continue jogging right past the photographers, past the medals, past the crowd cheering their name.

You'd stop them, wouldn't you?

You'd say: *"Wait, what are you doing? You finished! This is the moment!"*

Because who does that?

Who runs an entire marathon and doesn't stop at the finish line?

You'd never do that. Right?

Except, maybe you already have. Maybe we all have.

Why Some People Never Land

This is the danger of not recognizing your progress. If you don't take a moment to see where you are, to truly acknowledge what you've accomplished, you risk missing the entire point of the journey.

High achievers are especially prone to this. They accomplish something major, something they once believed was out of reach, and immediately their mind leaps ahead.

What's next? What's bigger? How do I keep going?

There's nothing wrong with ambition. But if you never allow yourself to feel your success, it will always seem just out of reach.

As we touched on in Chapter 4, Earl Nightingale defined success as "the progressive realization of a worthy ideal." That means success isn't just about the outcome; it's also about the movement toward it.

But if you never stop to recognize what you've done, your brain doesn't register the win. It keeps chasing. You'll feel like you're always behind, even when you've achieved something remarkable.

So, let's change that.

Let's make sure you don't just fly past your achievement.

Let's make sure you land.

Internalizing Success – Seeing the Transformation

Imagine, just for a moment, that you could go back in time and meet the version of yourself who first started this journey.

Picture that person. What were they afraid of? What did they not yet know? What seemed impossible to them back then?

Now, imagine telling them about where you are today.

Would they believe you? Would they even recognize you?

Would they say, *"No way. That's impossible. I could never do that."*

And yet… here you are.

Beyond the launch, the numbers, or crossing a finish line, the deeper measure of success is *who you became in the process.*

Take a moment and answer these questions:

- What did you doubt back then that you now know to be true?
- What skills, habits, or strengths have you built along the way?
- What part of your identity has evolved because of this experience?

This kind of transformation can sneak up on you. You get so focused on what you've done, you forget to recognize how much you've changed.

But when you truly see it, when you let that recognition sink in, something powerful happens.

You don't see success as an external achievement; you feel it as an internal shift.

That's when success becomes real.

That's when you land.

The *Ooh La La* Scale – The Transformation Edition

Success doesn't hit you all at once. It dawns on you.

To see where you are, check in with yourself on the Transformation Scale:

Level	Mindset	Action	Outcome
Ooh (Unrecognized Success)	"Yeah, I guess I accomplished that, but it's no big deal."	Downplaying wins, moving on without acknowledgment.	Never feels successful, always chasing.

Ooh La (Partial Recognition)	"I know I made progress, but I still have so much to do."	Acknowledging success but not fully internalizing it.	Feels proud for a moment but quickly moves to the next challenge.
Ooh La La (Fully Owning the Transformation)	"I see it. I've changed. I did this."	Taking time to reflect, acknowledge the internal and external shifts.	Feels grounded in success, uses it as fuel for the future.

Where do you fall right now?

- If you're still in *Ooh*, stop and take a moment. Sit with your success.
- If you're in *Ooh La*, slow down. You've worked hard to get here, don't let this moment slip by, acknowledge the shifts.
- If you're in *Ooh La La*, welcome to true success. You've landed.

Landing is about integration; it's when you let the success sink into your identity.

You're no longer someone chasing the goal. You're someone who lived it, achieved it, and became it.

You've gone from planning to practicing to being.

The Final Descent – Sticking the Landing

The planet is directly below now. The engines begin to adjust, the ship slows, and you brace for impact, not with fear but with the full awareness that this is the moment you've been working toward.

This is when all the effort, failures, breakthroughs, and relentless motion converge into something real.

For me, it means holding this finished book in my hands when it's published. That's my landing. The moment the idea becomes real.

For you, it might be completing your project, hitting your revenue goal, selling your art, finishing the race, or seeing the dream finally become reality.

Ooh La La. We made it!

This may feel like an ending, but it's really the launchpad for everything ahead.

But before anything else, before even thinking about what's next…

Recognize it. Feel it. Celebrate it, you landed.

2. CALIBRATING FOR CONTINUOUS SUCCESS

In 2009, a Navy SEAL team executed one of the most daring rescues in modern history: the rescue of Captain Richard Phillips from Somali pirates. The mission was as complex and dangerous as they come, yet it was carried out with precision. Three shots, three targets, zero mistakes. Phillips was brought home safely. By every measure, the operation was flawless.

Within hours of Phillips' rescue, they returned to base. The team was exhausted, running on adrenaline, but rest would have to wait. They gathered in a small room for what every SEAL team does, no matter the outcome: the debrief.

No one was above it. Rank didn't matter. Ego was checked at the door.

They walked through every detail of the mission:

- What was the original objective?
- What happened?
- Where did things go better than expected?
- Where did they almost fall apart?
- What needs to change next time?

Each team member spoke. Everyone was expected to take ownership of their part, both the wins and the mistakes.

A SEAL later explained it like this:

"We never let a win make us sloppy. A good outcome doesn't mean a perfect mission. We debrief every time, because that's how we stay alive, and how we get sharper."

Their success is a process, not luck. A commitment to continuous calibration, learning from each experience so the next one is smarter, cleaner, and more precise.

The So What

Most of us aren't operating in combat zones. But the principle still holds. Just because you've succeeded doesn't mean there's nothing left to learn. It's in the moments *after* the win, after the landing, that the most valuable insights emerge.

If you skip the debrief, you risk wasting the very experience you worked so hard to earn. You land, but you don't integrate. You achieve, but you don't evolve. You celebrate, but then move on with nothing sharpened or reinforced.

But when you take the time to reflect intentionally, to analyze, extract, and apply, you make your success stick. You move forward *smarter*.

Debriefing is what makes the landing meaningful.

It's the step that transforms a completed mission into a launchpad for future growth.

The After-Action Review (AAR): A Framework for Growth

The military refers to it as an After-Action Review (AAR). It's structured, simple, and endlessly adaptable. You don't need a war room or tactical mission to use it. All you need is a willingness to stop, reflect, and learn.

Here's the four-part process SEALs (and now, you) can use:

Step 1: What Was Supposed to Happen?

Before you can understand the outcome, revisit the original mission.

What was your goal when you started this journey?

Were you launching a business, writing a book, hitting a health target, or leading a major creative project? What were the specific benchmarks you hoped to hit? What was your timeline?

Getting clear on your intent anchors the rest of your review. It gives you something to measure against: your standard, not someone else's.

Examples:

- Marie set out to build a wellness center. She had clear incremental goals: gaining her first five loyal clients, launching transformative programs, growing her team, and ultimately, establishing a thriving community hub.
- Alex aimed to build a financial education platform, setting a target of 10,000 subscribers within a year.

Start your debrief by asking:

- What did I want to accomplish?
- What was the timeline I expected?
- What did success mean to me at the start?

Revisiting your original intent brings clarity to the debrief process. This is about measuring progress against what you set out to achieve, not against arbitrary external standards.

Step 2: What Actually Happened?

Now, compare your plan to reality. This is your mission report.

- Did you meet your goals?

- What surprises or challenges came up?
- Were there external factors (like market shifts or resource limitations)?
- Or internal ones (like mindset, motivation, or execution)?
- Did you pivot? Did those pivots help?

Examples:

- Marie was in a similar situation to Emma, whom we just met in the last chapter. She exceeded expectations in building strong client connections but struggled with delegation and felt stretched too thin.
- Alex hit his subscriber target but realized his overall engagement numbers were flatter than projected.

You can't optimize what you don't analyze. Defining what really happened, celebrations and setbacks alike, lays the groundwork for powerful, informed progress.

Step 3: What Went Right, and What Could Improve?

This is where you mine the gold.

- What systems, habits, or decisions worked well?
- What challenges kept recurring?
- Were there inefficiencies, distractions, or unnecessary struggles?
- Where did you waste energy or overcomplicate things?

Examples:

- Marie's biggest realization? Her business could have grown faster if she had embraced leadership sooner, rather than trying to handle every aspect herself.
- Alex discovered that focusing solely on subscriber growth was limiting his bigger vision; true success meant deepening audience trust and engagement.

This kind of honest self-reflection is what separates those who plateau from those who continue to level up.

Step 4: What Will You Do Differently Next Time?

This is your pivot.

Take everything you've just reflected on and distill it into one clear takeaway for future action.

- What mindset shift will you make?
- What habit will you build, or stop?
- What strategy will you refine?
- What system needs an upgrade?

Examples:

- Marie's key takeaway? She needed to step back from day-to-day tasks and step into leadership. Instead of just running her wellness business, she needed to structure it for sustainability and growth. She decided to bring in a team, delegate operational tasks, and focus on optimizing the impact of her center.
- For Alex, the biggest shift was realizing that engagement and impact mattered more than just hitting numbers. He refined his strategy to focus on deeper audience relationships, planning more interactive content and partnerships that aligned with his mission.

This process is not only reflection but strategic refinement. Each subsequent step becomes stronger because you chose to learn from the last.

Your Post-Mission Debrief: A Personal Exercise

Grab your journal, a blank document, or hit record on a voice memo. Use these four questions to guide your reflection:

1. What was your original goal?
   - What were you trying to accomplish?
   - What milestones and timeline did you set?
2. What actually happened?
   - What went as planned? What shifted?
   - What challenges or wins emerged unexpectedly?
3. What were your biggest strengths or struggles?
   - What mindsets or behaviors helped you succeed?
   - Were there inefficiencies or blind spots?
4. What's one key adjustment for the future?
   - What will you change or refine next time?
   - What lesson are you ready to lock in?

Tips to Elevate Your Debrief

- Do it with a witness.
  A coach, mentor, or peer can help you see what you might miss and hold you accountable for the learning.

- Use your data.
  Look at the numbers: habits, revenue, time invested, outcomes. Measure both what you did and what it led to.

- Be radically honest but judgment-free.
  It's about clarity, without being hard on yourself.

- Celebrate the wins.
  Say them out loud. Write them down. Let your nervous system feel what it's like to succeed.

A Personal Note: My Own Debrief

As I was writing this very book, I found myself in my version of a mission debrief. I came into the process with a plan and a detailed outline, but I had no idea how much I'd be challenged, stretched, and changed along the way.

There were moments I thought I had nothing new to say… and days when the words flowed as if they'd always been waiting.

The biggest lessons?

- Patience: Writing this book stretched me in ways I didn't expect. Delays, rewrites, and long pauses became part of the journey. Each one reminded me that timing has its own wisdom, and the right pieces fall into place when you're ready for them.

- Authenticity: I spent time studying other authors and frameworks, but the turning point came when I stopped chasing someone else's style. The work came alive when I leaned into my own experiences and voice. That's when the pages started to feel true.

- Trust the Process: This book took shape draft by draft, evolving as I did. Some chapters fell away; others surprised me by demanding more space. Letting it unfold instead of forcing perfection gave the final version a depth I couldn't have planned.

So, as you reflect on your progress, whether you're debriefing a business success, a creative milestone, or a personal transformation, remember: clarity doesn't always come before action. Often, it appears because of this.

The Next Step: Exploring the New World You've Landed On

Now that we've landed and analyzed the mission, a new question emerges: What does this new world look like?

You've landed somewhere your past self only dreamed of. Take the time to fully see what you've built and truly feel it.

In the next section, we'll explore how to fully embrace, appreciate, and thrive in this new environment. You've worked hard to get here. Now, it's time to truly see the world you've built.

3. EXPLORING YOUR NEW PLANET

The Shift in Perspective – Seeing the World with New Eyes

There's an old fable about a traveler who spent years searching for a legendary city. The stories promised golden streets, sky-touching towers, and an endless land of opportunity. He weathered storms, endured hunger, and faced countless setbacks. But finally, one day, he saw it on the horizon.

As he stepped through the grand gates, something unexpected happened. The city was real, just as the legends had said. But instead of marveling at its golden streets, he found himself fixated on something else: the people. Some were thriving, building businesses, creating art, and expanding the city's influence. Others wandered, unsure of what came next now that they had arrived.

It wasn't the city that determined their experience. It was how they saw it.

That's the shift that happens when you reach a long-pursued goal. At first, you see the external achievement: the book published, the business thriving, the finish line crossed. But almost immediately, your perspective changes. The things you once feared shrink. The possibilities you couldn't see before come into view. Most importantly, you realize you're no longer the same person who began this journey.

This shift in perspective is subtle but powerful. It's the realization that the challenges you once feared are now just part of the landscape. It's understanding that while this may have been your biggest goal before, it's now just the beginning of something even greater.

When you land on a new planet, everything is unfamiliar. The gravity feels different, the air is strange, and the terrain is both exciting and unpredictable. Your instincts may urge you to rush ahead and figure out what's next. But before you move, pause.

Look around. What do you see now that you couldn't see before? What do you know now that your past self didn't? It's an entirely new reality, no longer a finish line.

The New Reality – Opportunities and Challenges in a Foreign Land

Every new world has its terrain. When astronauts land on a new planet, they immediately assess the environment. What resources are available? What potential lies beneath the surface? What risks demand attention?

You're in the same position. Now that you've arrived, you're seeing things that weren't visible from the outside.

New Opportunities

One of the most exciting parts of reaching this stage is discovering what wasn't available to you before. Just as a new planet might reveal rare minerals or new elements, success exposes you to possibilities that didn't exist when you were at the beginning.

- Momentum Attracts Momentum – Now that you've built something, people take notice. You might find that partnerships, collaborations, or new ventures come to you naturally.
- Resources You Didn't Have Before – More capital, stronger networks, deeper expertise; these are assets that can now be leveraged.
- New Creative Sparks – With the pressure of survival lifted, your mind is free to explore new ideas, innovations, and directions.

Marie began with a simple goal: to sign a few clients and create meaningful wellness programs. Her focus was practical and personal. Back then, success meant filling her schedule and making a difference one client at a time.

Now, standing inside her thriving wellness center, everything has changed. Her vision has grown beyond what she once imagined. She sees new possibilities, like partnering with corporations for large-scale wellness initiatives, creating certification programs to train others, and expanding her impact in ways that weren't visible from the starting line.

Alex's journey started small, too. His aim was clear: build a financial education platform and reach 10,000 subscribers. He poured himself into every detail. Each video, comment, and milestone mattered deeply.

But once he hit that target, his perspective shifted. It wasn't just about numbers anymore. It was about creating real impact. With this clarity came fresh ideas. Building an interactive community, designing online courses, and hosting live workshops. The more he grew, the more opportunities appeared, ones he couldn't have seen in those early days.

These new opportunities weren't missing before. Alex and Marie simply weren't in the position to see them yet.

What new possibilities have opened for you now that you've arrived?

New Challenges

But just as a new planet reveals treasures, it also presents new challenges.

- The Weight of Expectation – When you're just starting, expectations are low. But once you've built something, an invisible pressure kicks in: to grow, to sustain, to never slip. The fear of losing ground can become its burden.
- The Complexity of Growth – Scaling is different from building. The problems you solve now aren't the same as before. Instead of struggling for resources, you may be managing demand, making tough decisions, or navigating unexpected complications.
- The Fear of Letting Go – What got you here won't necessarily get you where you want to go next. The hardest part? You may have to stop doing things that once felt essential.

Marie quickly found herself in a role different from what she expected. She was no longer just serving clients; she was leading a team, managing operations, and shaping the future of her business. The pressure to grow and maintain momentum was real, and it brought with it an entirely new set of challenges.

The biggest shift? Learning to let go of control and step into leadership, an identity that once felt distant but was now necessary.

For Alex, the challenges were different but just as real.

His platform had momentum, but that momentum came with demands. The systems that once worked—editing every video himself, replying to every message—were no longer sustainable. He had to confront a brutal truth: doing everything alone was no longer an option.

To move forward, he needed to delegate, automate, and build trust in others to help carry the vision.

The growth they had both fought for had arrived. But it didn't make things easier; it made things more complex.

And that's the tradeoff of elevation: it expands your view but also your responsibility.

Now that you've arrived, what new obstacles do you see?

Thriving in a New Environment – The Transition from Striving to Living

For so long, the focus was on getting here. Now, it's about being here.

You've been in survival mode, pushing, grinding, and proving yourself. But you're no longer on the outside looking in. This world is yours now.

So, what does it mean to truly live in this space?

- Shift from "Proving" to "Owning" – You don't have to justify your success. You belong here.
- Master the Environment – Instead of reacting, start intentionally designing your days, your work, and your priorities based on this new reality.
- Lean into Expansion – Now that you're established, how can you maximize your impact, explore deeper, and use what you've built to create even greater value?

There's a moment in every astronaut's journey when they stop looking at their new planet as "foreign" and start calling it "home." That's where you are now.

This isn't a transition you rush. Take time to understand the new environment before deciding what's next.

Practical Exercise: From Arrival to Ownership

You've landed, but now it's time to live here, to shift from proving yourself to fully embodying this new reality.

Use the following questions to help integrate this transition. It's about grounding yourself in who you've become and choosing how you want to lead from here.

1. What's different about your world now? What do you have access to, see, or understand that was impossible before?
2. What's different about you? How have your mindset, confidence, or abilities evolved?

3. What are the new opportunities in this space? What resources, people, or ideas have appeared since you reached this milestone?
4. What are the new challenges? What new obstacles exist that didn't before?
5. How will you shift from survival to thriving? What needs to change in your approach to fully embrace this new stage?

You've landed. You've explored. You've begun to understand the terrain.

But the journey isn't over. The next chapter is about reinvention. Now that you've reached this point, how do you evolve into the next version of yourself and your mission?

OOH *LA LA* HIGHLIGHTS

STEP 10: LAND WITH INTENTION

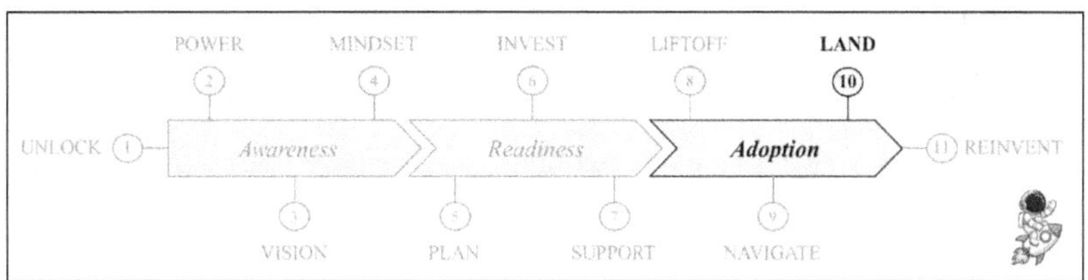

MISSION BRIEF

A key part of success is to recognize when you've arrived. High achievers often move on too quickly, missing the significance of their progress. True success comes from internalizing growth, celebrating achievements, and embracing the transformation that happened along the way.

CRITICAL SYSTEMS CHECK

- The Risk of Flying Past Success
  - Achievers often shift to the next goal too quickly, never fully acknowledging what they've accomplished.
  - If you don't internalize success, it will always feel out of reach, like you're still chasing something, even after you've won.
- The Transformation Test – Are You Seeing the Change?
  - Think back to the person you were at the beginning of this journey. Would they believe where you are now?
  - Growth is about who you've become in the process.
- The *Ooh La La* Scale – The Transformation Edition
  - *Ooh* – Downplaying wins, feeling like it's not a big deal.
  - *Ooh La* – Acknowledging progress but quickly shifting to the next challenge.
  - *Ooh La La* – Fully embracing the transformation, recognizing and celebrating the journey.

PILOT'S REFLECTION

1. Are you truly recognizing your success, or already chasing the next thing?
2. How have you changed since you started this journey?
3. What's one way you can celebrate and integrate your achievement before moving forward?

NEXT COORDINATES

You've stuck the landing; now it's time to chart your next adventure. In the final chapter, we'll explore how to build on your success and intentionally shape your next move.

CHAPTER 11

•

REINVENT - THE JOURNEY CONTINUES

1. YOUR NEW VANTAGE POINT

After everything, the struggle, the climb, the breakthroughs, you've reached the summit of your growth curve.

Take a moment. Breathe it in.

From this vantage point, the view is spectacular. The obstacles that once felt like mountains are now tiny specs in the distance. The fear that once shadowed every decision has been replaced by experience. The self-doubt that whispered, *"Who do you think you are?"* has been drowned out by the quiet confidence of someone who's done the work.

This is *Ooh La La*, you have arrived.

But as your eyes adjust to this new height, another realization begins to dawn: the journey isn't over. Standing still is not an option.

Yes, you deserve a pause. Take the time to celebrate, reflect, and fully own your success. But once the champagne has been popped and the confetti settles, an inevitable question begins to rise: *"What comes next?"*

For some, the answer is clear. They already feel the pull toward the next project, the next vision, the next bold leap. But for others, and maybe this is you, the clarity doesn't come so easily. There's pride in what you've built but also a strange sense of restlessness, despite everything you've accomplished.

Here's what I've learned: if you don't intentionally decide what's next, the world will choose for you. And that's where things can start to slip.

The *Ooh La La* Trap

Wait a second. The *Ooh La La* Trap? How can being in the *Ooh La La* state be a problem? Isn't this exactly where we've all been trying to get?

It is. And it feels incredible. You've hit your stride. You're in flow. You're no longer in survival mode. You've built something that works. The pressure has eased, the results are real, and for once, you feel like you've arrived.

But here's the trap:

If you're not careful, *Ooh La La* quietly slides into *Ooh La…* and eventually, back into just *Ooh*.

Let's break it down:

- *Ooh La La* is where everything clicks. You're energized, aligned, and creating meaningful results.
- Then comes *Ooh La...* It still looks like success from the outside, but something's changed. You're repeating what worked before, not reinventing. The spark is dimming. You're optimizing the past instead of designing the future.
- Stay there long enough, and you reach *Ooh*. Passion fades. Innovation stalls. Results slip. You're still in motion, but it's downhill… in the dreaded Decline phase.

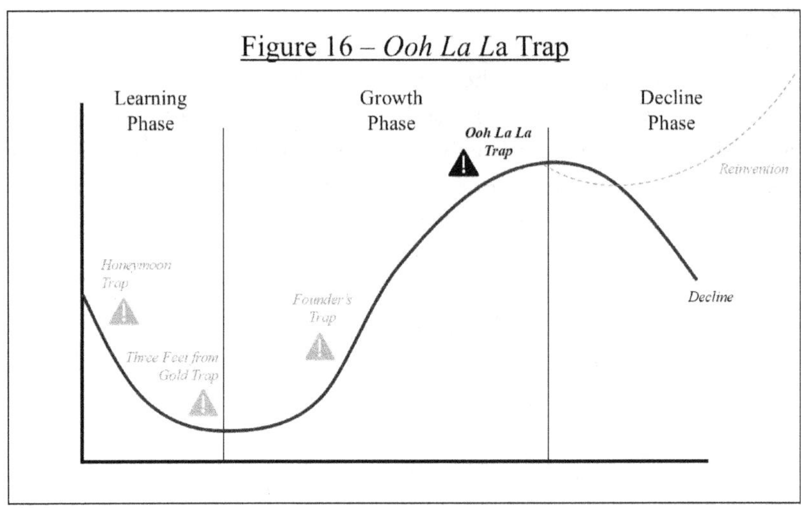

Figure 16 – *Ooh La La* Trap

It's a Slow Fade, Not a Sudden Fall

The hardest part about this descent is that it doesn't feel like a crash. It feels more like a plateau.

There's no alarm bell. No big failure. No crisis moment.

It shows up in subtler ways:

- You feel less excited about ideas that once lit you up.
- You catch yourself just going through the motions.
- You tell yourself, *"It's still working,"* even though, deep down, you know something's off.

It's like staying in a relationship that's "fine."

You still show up. You still smile. But something's missing. There's less fire, less imagination, less connection. Nothing is broken, but nothing is growing.

And that's how it happens to people. Quietly. Gradually.

Not with a bang but with a fade.

The Blockbuster Problem Isn't Just a Business Story

You've probably heard the Blockbuster story before.

At its peak in 2004, Blockbuster had over 9,000 stores and billions in revenue. It was a household name, a cultural institution. On the surface, it looked invincible.

Then, in 2008, Netflix approached them with a partnership offer.

Blockbuster declined. Why change what was working?

By 2010, they had filed for bankruptcy. Netflix had already reinvented the model and the market.

This story has been told many times. However, what's often overlooked is this: Blockbuster wasn't failing when it made its worst decision. They were winning. They were profitable. They were dominant.

That's what makes the trap so dangerous.

It wasn't complacency that took them down; it was confidence in a model that had already stopped evolving. The illusion of success numbed them to the signals that change was coming. They didn't adapt because they didn't feel the urgency to adapt.

That was fifteen years ago.

Back then, you could fade slowly. Decline unfolded over the years. There was room, dangerous room, to delay reinvention.

But not anymore.

Today, the world moves faster. The slow fade still happens, but now, it can take you from top of mind to almost forgotten in the span of just a couple of seasons.

Just look at Peloton.

At the height of the pandemic, Peloton was everywhere. Their bikes were sold out for months. Their instructors were celebrities. The brand became a movement, a lifestyle, a daily ritual in millions of homes.

But as the world reopened, momentum shifted.

Sales slowed. Inventory swelled. Stock prices fell. Leadership changed. The energy that once surrounded the brand began to dissipate, not overnight, but fast.

Peloton didn't collapse. But it faded. And it faded far more quickly than Blockbuster ever did.

Now, the company is working hard to reinvent itself. They're expanding their app, opening up access beyond their hardware, and shifting from being a luxury product to a broader digital platform.

Whether that reinvention succeeds remains to be seen.

However, the message is clear: what once worked will not always continue to work. And in today's world, holding onto the past, even a successful past, can become a liability faster than ever before.

That's the danger. Not visible failure but the slow, quiet erosion of relevance—a risk that threatens not just companies but people, too.

Reinvention Is the Antidote

This is why reinvention matters.

Not just to stay relevant. Not just to protect what you've built. But to stay ahead of the curve, before the curve leaves you behind.

Reinvention is the conscious decision to grow again. It's the act of disrupting your comfort before the world does it for you. It means being bold enough to ask, "What needs to evolve?" even when things appear to be working.

The most effective reinvention begins when things are still good, when momentum is still on your side, and you still have the capacity to lead the change, not react to it.

- It's the entrepreneur who refines their offer before the market shifts.
- It's the creator who experiments with new formats before their audience gets bored.
- It's the leader who reimagines team culture before burnout starts to spread.

You can make reinvention a mindset or a way of operating by asking yourself:

- What needs to evolve to keep me aligned and growing?
- What am I holding onto that used to serve me but no longer does?
- What possibilities am I ignoring because I'm comfortable?

We can't control the rate of change. But we can control how we respond to it.

Reinvention is about staying connected to your vision, your purpose, and your future. It's how you keep yourself in motion instead of slipping into maintenance mode.

Reinvention as a Habit

The most successful people and organizations don't reinvent themselves once. They build reinvention into their identity.

- They evolve while things are still working.
- They challenge assumptions before the market does.
- They disrupt themselves on purpose.

Think of:

- Beyoncé has redefined her identity again and again, from Destiny's Child to solo icon, from mainstream pop star to cultural force and business powerhouse.
- Steve Jobs, who turned Apple from a personal computer company into a global innovation and design empire.
- Taylor Swift, who moved from country to pop to indie-folk, reimagined her business model and deepened her audience connection at every stage.
- Dwayne "The Rock" Johnson has evolved from wrestling celebrity to Hollywood star to entrepreneur and global brand.
- Oprah, who continually transforms from daytime host to media mogul to wellness advocate to thought leader.

What all of them have in common is this: they didn't wait for the world to tell them to change. They chose it. They made reinvention a rhythm.

Now, It's Your Turn

This next section is your reinvention lab.

We'll map the phases of your past growth, identify where you might be repeating instead of evolving, and start building your next launchpad—not because you need to but because you're ready.

You've already proven that you can grow, adapt, and rise.

Now, it's time to do it again, not from a place of struggle or survival but from strength.

Because reinvention starts with vision, with choice, and it starts with you.

So, the real question is this:

What will the next version of you become?

2: RECOGNIZE THE PATTERN

At this stage, it's common to look outward for answers, seeking advice, analyzing market trends, and trying to figure out what "makes the most sense" for the next move.

But the key to sustained success is more about internal alignment than external pressure.

Your best next step will come from aligning with who you've become, what you truly value, and the impact you want to make going forward.

To move forward with intention, you need to do two things:

- Step 1: Look back at the growth that brought you here.
- Step 2: Look forward at what's calling you next.

This section is Step 1: Look Back—because before we map out your next chapter, we need to connect the dots from the chapters that shaped you.

Step 1. Look Back – Recognizing Growth & Connecting the Dots

At the start of this book, we focused on Awareness, unlocking the power that was already within you. You learned that success is about tapping into your intrinsic motivation and discovering what truly drives you, not external validation.

You crafted a vision, a clear destination that served as your guiding star. You mapped out where you were, identified the gap between your present and future, and made a Case for Change so compelling that it fueled your drive to move forward.

Then came Readiness, preparing for liftoff. You built your Mission Blueprint, identified the key factors that would accelerate your success, and anticipated obstacles that could slow you down. You strengthened your mindset, sharpened your skills, and assembled a support system to ensure you had the right people and structures in place.

With the groundwork set, it was time for Adoption—you launched. You experienced the Honeymoon Phase, the thrill of early wins, and then faced resistance, those moments when doubt crept in, and progress felt slow. But you pushed through. You kept going even when motivation faded.

Through it all, you adapted, optimized, and expanded. You reached the Growth Phase, where momentum worked in your favor, and you mastered the art of sustaining success. Then, you reached the top, landed, and took in the new reality.

And now?

Your vantage point has changed. You are no longer the person who started this journey.

But here's something important to recognize: this isn't your first cycle of growth.

Reflect on your life: your career, relationships, and personal growth. Haven't you been here before? Haven't you faced challenges, evolved, and reached new heights? You've likely experienced multiple growth cycles already, even if you didn't have a framework for them at the time.

This book may have guided you through a transformation, but it's just one chapter in a much bigger story, your story. And just as you've navigated previous cycles, you'll navigate the next one too. The patterns, the struggles, the breakthroughs; they've been there all along.

So before thinking about what's next, take a moment to honor how far you've come. Reflect on the versions of yourself that existed before this one. Every step, even the hard ones, shaped the person you are today.

Why I'm Sharing My Cycles of Growth

Before we dive into mapping your journey, I want to share a few chapters from mine. Not because the path I took is one to copy but because it might help you see your own more clearly. We often overlook our transformation because we're so close to it. Sometimes, seeing someone else connect the dots gives us the language, structure, or spark to connect our own.

Looking back, my journey has been a series of growth curves, each one shaping the next. At first, every transition felt like a leap of faith, a mix of gut instinct, curiosity, and a willingness to figure things out on the fly. However, over time, I began to recognize patterns and learn how to make intentional moves that aligned with what energized me.

Not every step was planned, but each one built on the last, and what once felt like "just trying things" became a deliberate path forward.

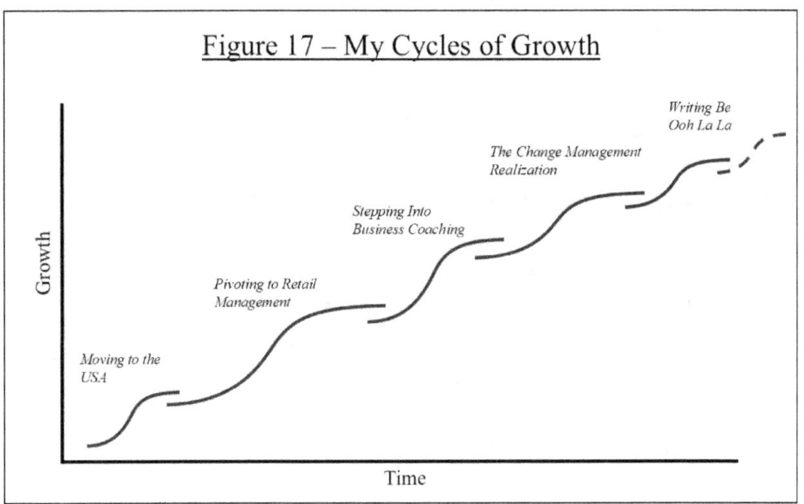

Figure 17 – My Cycles of Growth

- Moving to the USA – A Crash Course in Culture, Coffee, and Career

When I moved from France to the United States, everything felt new, exciting, overwhelming, and unfamiliar in the best and strangest ways. It was a major leap into a world with different expectations, rhythms, and ways of communicating. And yes, even the coffee was confusing.

Back home, a tiny, bold espresso was a ritual: concentrated, intentional, just a few perfect sips. But in the U.S., I found myself in diners where my mug was constantly refilled with something lukewarm and endless. It felt like a metaphor for everything: bigger, faster, more, but not always better.

Don't worry, I've since found the right places in America to get a proper coffee. That journey, like so many others, just took a little time and curiosity.

My first job in technical sales development, working with French companies as they expanded into new markets, threw me into unfamiliar environments. I didn't always know what I was doing, but I kept showing up, translating what I knew into new contexts, and learning to adapt. It was scrappy. It was unpredictable. It was foundational.

That experience taught me how to navigate ambiguity, stay resourceful, and grow by doing, even when the path was not yet clear.

- Pivoting to Retail Management – From "Temporary Job" to Personal Transformation

Retail wasn't part of the plan. I took the job thinking it would be temporary, something to bridge the gap while I figured out what was next. But then Michelle happened. (If you've read Chapter 2, you already know.)

Michelle saw something in me I hadn't yet seen in myself. She challenged me, championed me, and helped me discover a deeper passion I didn't know I had: leadership, coaching, growth.

Initially, I was focused on ensuring things ran smoothly. Managing a store. Hitting numbers. But once I began leaning into people development, supporting my team, helping others rise, I lit up. That spark grew into a calling.

This cycle taught me that what starts as "just a job" can sometimes become your most defining breakthrough. It was the first time I saw myself not just as someone trying to succeed but as someone capable of helping others succeed, too.

- Becoming a Business Coach – Scaling Impact with Intention

Coaching wasn't a career change; it was the natural evolution of everything I'd been building. I had seen the impact of leadership and development from the inside. Now, I wanted to help others grow at scale and with strategy.

There were growing pains, of course. I had to find my voice, build trust, and translate years of experience into tools others could use. But with every client, I got clearer. I started building my own frameworks, sharpening my process, and grounding my work in both empathy and strategy.

This was the first move I made with full intention. I knew it was the right fit. I had the passion, the skills, and now, the focus to turn it into something sustainable.

Coaching allowed me to help leaders not just build businesses but become the kind of people who could lead them with clarity and confidence.

That's when I knew: *This work is meaningful, and it fits me.*

- Embracing Change Management – Expanding the Toolkit, Deepening the Impact

As I coached and consulted with more entrepreneurs and leaders, I began stepping into work that required a different lens: broader, more complex, and often involving whole teams or organizations in transition.

It took me a while to realize it, but I had been doing change management all along. I just hadn't been calling it that. Every transformation I supported, every growth challenge, every pivot, every leadership reset, was about guiding people from where they were to where they wanted to go.

Once I recognized that, I leaned in more intentionally. I began refining my approach, seeking out frameworks that could support bigger shifts, and adding new tools to my toolkit. It was about owning what I was already doing and doing it better.

This phase brought structure to my instincts and strategy to my experience. I was learning how to guide transformation with more clarity and confidence.

- Writing This Book – Pulling the Thread Through It All

Writing this book was not really a new chapter but more of a way to connect all the chapters that came before it.

At first, it felt overwhelming. I had stories, tools, and insights but no clear shape. There were plenty of *Ooh* moments: staring at the screen, wondering if any of it was worth sharing. But I kept going, one sentence at a time.

Eventually, I began to see the patterns. The way each experience built on the last. The way growth showed up: sometimes loud, sometimes subtle, always teaching. And I realized that sharing this wasn't just for me. It was for anyone else navigating their own messy, meaningful evolution.

This book is a way of giving back. A way to take everything I've learned and everything I'm still learning and offer it as a companion for others on the path. Not a prescription but a provocation: to grow with more clarity, curiosity, intention, and a whole lot of *Ooh La La.*

None of these cycles was clean. None were perfectly mapped. But each time, I got a little more intentional, a little more aware of the process I was in. What began as a series of reactions eventually became a rhythm, my rhythm.

Now, it's your turn.
What have your growth cycles looked like?
What seasons shaped you most?

And what could become possible if you chose to grow, on purpose, from here?

3: YOUR PAST HOLDS THE MAP

Your Turn: Map Your S-Curves

Now that you've seen how my cycles unfolded, it's your turn. This is the heart of Step 1: looking back to uncover your transformation patterns.

Grab a blank piece of paper (no electronics needed for this). Draw a series of S-curves, just like the ones in the template below.

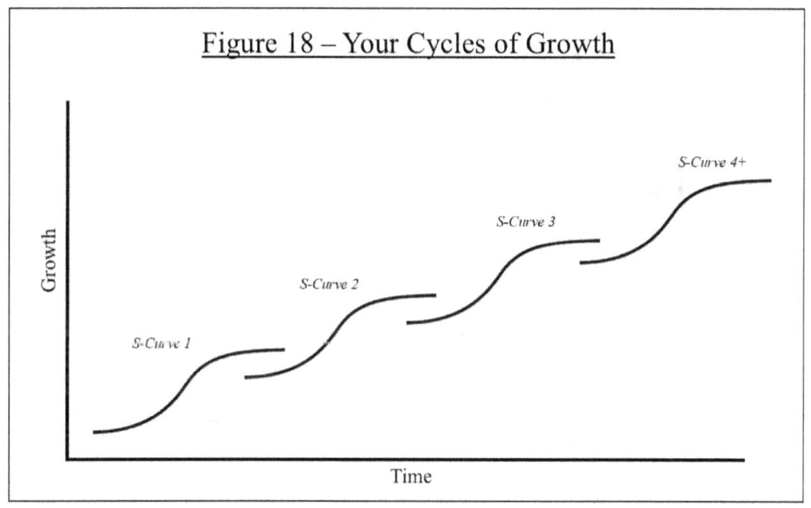

Now, think through your journey:

- Label each curve with a significant phase of growth in your life: career shifts, personal reinventions, challenges you've overcome.
- Note how long each cycle lasted; some of mine spanned fifteen years, with a couple of mini cycles within them, and others less than three.
- Recognize that not all S-curves are glamorous. Some were *Ooh La La* (high momentum, thriving), some were *Ooh La* (interrupted, but valuable), and some were just *Ooh* (less than ideal, but still growth).
- Identify the transitions. What patterns emerge? Did one cycle naturally lead to another, or were some interrupted?

- Acknowledge the tough ones. Some of your cycles may feel like failures, but were they, really? Or were they essential experiences that shaped who you are today? Growth doesn't always look pretty, but it's still growth.

Questions to Guide Your Reflection

- How have you grown?
- What strengths have you developed along the way?
- What lessons have reshaped your understanding of success?

Once you've mapped it out, take a step back. Look at your life's cycles in one visual snapshot.

Now, take a deep breath. You have more experience, resilience, and clarity than you may have realized.

Recognizing Your Patterns

As you analyze your S-curves, you might start to notice some recurring themes. Here are a few examples of common patterns:

- The Builder: Every Growth Phase for you has involved creating something from scratch, whether a business, a program, or a movement. You thrive in the early stages but sometimes struggle with maintaining long-term momentum.
- The Problem-Solver: Your S-curves are marked by moments of crisis or challenge, where you stepped in, fixed something, and then moved on. You get energy from tackling big problems but might find yourself needing new challenges once things stabilize.
- The Reinventor: Your cycles show a pattern of continuous reinvention: shifting industries, roles, or even entire career paths. You not only accept change, you actively chase it.
- The Growth Seeker: Your S-curves tend to end when things get too comfortable. Once you've mastered something, you're ready to move on to the next challenge. If you're not growing, you feel stuck.
- The Guide: Your fulfillment comes from helping others grow. Each S-Curve has involved some form of mentorship, coaching, or teaching, whether formally or informally.

- The Deep Diver: Instead of jumping from curve to curve quickly, your cycles are long, sometimes spanning decades. Your growth comes from digging deeper into a craft or mission, refining mastery over time.

Your journey might not fit perfectly into any single category, and that's the whole point. It's uniquely yours. The aim isn't to squeeze into a set mold but to understand the patterns that have shaped your growth. When you take a step back and examine your S-Curves, you start to uncover what energizes your best work, where you flourish, and what wears you down. These insights can help guide you toward where you're meant to head next.

Your past doesn't dictate your future, but it does offer a powerful roadmap. It reveals what excites you, what challenges push you forward, and where your strengths naturally shine.

Now that you see the cycle for what it is, you have something even more powerful: the ability to move forward with more clarity.

You have surfaced your past patterns and reclaimed the lessons; it's time to get intentional about what comes next.

4. CHOOSE YOUR NEXT GROWTH PATH

You've looked back. You've mapped your growth. Now it's time for Step 2—Looking Forward.

This is where we reconnect with your vision and align it with who you've become.

Step 2: Look Forward – Revisit Your Case for Change

At the beginning of this book, you defined your Case for Change: a clear vision of where you were and where you wanted to go. You mapped your From-To statement, identifying what needed to shift to step into the next level of your growth. Now, revisit that work with a fresh perspective and hard-earned clarity.

Look back at Chapter 3, where you outlined your transformation.

- Does your original vision still hold?
- Have your experiences expanded your view of what is possible?
- Does your "To" destination still excite and challenge you, or does it need refinement?

Sometimes, our original goal was just a stepping stone toward something bigger. At other times, the journey itself shifts our priorities, revealing new opportunities that we couldn't have seen from the starting line.

Now, ask yourself:

- Has my "why" changed?
- What is pulling me forward now?
- If I were to rewrite my From-To statement based on everything I've learned, what would it say today?

Your next move should align with who you've become, not just who you were when you wrote the plan months or years ago. This reflection will help guide you to the right path in the assessment ahead.

Your best move forward will come from clarity about what truly matters to you right now, not external expectations.

The Crossroad – Three Paths Forward

At this moment, you are at a critical crossroads. Three distinct paths stretch before you, each leading to a different future.

Some will choose to stay and optimize, not by standing still but by deepening and refining what they've built. Others will scale and expand, using their success as a launchpad for greater reach and impact. And then some will explore a new challenge, ready to embark on a fresh journey and embrace reinvention at its core.

Let's explore how each of these paths might unfold through the journeys of some familiar travelers we've encountered:

Path 1: Stay & Optimize – Marie's Evolution

Marie set out with a mission: to create a wellness center that empowers people to live healthier lives. She has now built a thriving business, with a dedicated community and meaningful impact. But instead of chasing aggressive expansion, she chooses a different approach: deepening her impact.

For Marie, staying means:

- Refining her business model to make her services even more valuable.
- Focusing on client transformation rather than chasing numbers.
- Improving efficiency so she can spend more time on what truly matters.

She chooses to optimize rather than expand, ensuring long-term sustainability while preserving the personal, community-driven nature of her work.

Who this path is for:

For creators, builders, and changemakers who love what they've built and want to deepen it. This is for those who care more about crafting meaning than chasing scale, who want to refine their work, protect their energy, and keep showing up with heart and excellence. Whether you're running a wellness studio, writing a newsletter, leading a team, or growing a personal practice, this path is about going deeper, not necessarily bigger.

Path 2: Scale & Expand – Alex's Ascent

Alex built a financial education platform from scratch. His initial goal was simple: launch a YouTube channel and reach 10,000 subscribers. But once he hit that milestone, he realized he wanted more; greater reach and the chance to build something bigger.

For him, scaling means:

- Turning his brand into a broader platform by expanding beyond YouTube.
- Building a team to help him manage content, engagement, and strategy.
- Creating multiple income streams through online courses, books, and live events.

Alex knows that the work he's doing is meaningful, and scaling allows him to serve more people, increase his influence, and make a greater difference.

Who this path is for:

For those who feel momentum and are ready to multiply it. If you're energized by impact, excited to reach more people, and eager to grow your vision into something bigger than yourself, this path is yours. It's for the visionaries, educators, content creators, and builders who want to move from solo success to scalable systems, whether through platforms, teams, products, or partnerships.

Path 3: Explore a New Challenge – Emma's Next Mission

Emma had built a multi-million-dollar business, but something inside her stirred. She wasn't done growing. She had two choices: keep running her company as it was or step into an entirely new challenge.

For Emma, the answer was clear: It was time to reinvent again, from scratch.

Instead of continuing to lead her business, she decided to sell it, allowing someone else to take the reins while she embarked on a new journey. But this time, she wasn't just growing another business; she was helping others do it.

Her new challenge? Launching an incubator for service-based businesses, guiding entrepreneurs through the exact growth journey she had navigated. Instead of managing clients directly, she was now coaching, mentoring, and investing in early-stage founders, equipping them with the tools and strategies to grow beyond their own limits. Recognizing the struggle entrepreneurs face in the "do-it-all" trap, she knew she was uniquely positioned to offer practical, hands-on guidance. Emma's reinvention was about using everything she had learned to create a bigger impact than ever before.

Who this path is for:

For the curious souls who've done something meaningful and now feel called to something new. Maybe you've built a business, launched a creative career, or run a team, and now you're asking: What else am I capable of? This path is for those who are ready to pivot, evolve, or reinvent, from founders to facilitators, from performers to mentors, from doing the work to shaping the next wave. You're not starting over. You're building forward, using everything you've learned to create something even more aligned.

The Three Paths – Which One Calls You?

Each of these paths we discovered leads to growth but in different ways. Which one feels most aligned with your vision, values, and strengths?

How to Use This Assessment:

- Reflect on your answers to the key questions. Which path resonates with you the most?
- Consider the benefits and challenges. Are you ready for what each option requires?
- Look at the examples. Which one feels closest to your journey?

CHOOSING YOUR NEXT PATH: A SELF-ASSESSMENT GUIDE

Stay & Optimize

Description	**You love what you've built and want to refine it for deeper impact, efficiency, and sustainability.**
Questions to Ask	- Am I deeply fulfilled by what I'm doing? - Do I see untapped potential in my current work? - Can I make things run more smoothly or effectively?
Focus	Deepening impact, improving systems, optimizing processes, increasing efficiency
Benefits	- Strengthens core foundations - Creates long-term sustainability - Allows for mastery of your craft
Challenges	- Can feel less "exciting" than starting something new - Requires patience and focus on details
Example	Marie – Strengthening her wellness center, refining her programs, and making operations more seamless

Scale & Expand

Description	**Your work has gained traction, and you're ready to reach a wider audience, increase revenue, or build a larger enterprise.**
Questions to Ask	- Is my current success scalable? - Am I excited about reaching more people or markets? - Do I have the right systems and team to support growth?
Focus	Expanding reach, increasing revenue, leveraging momentum, and building infrastructure
Benefits	- Increases income and impact - Opens doors to larger opportunities - Builds long-term wealth and brand presence
Challenges	- Requires leadership, delegation, and system-building - Risk of overextending without a proper strategy

Example	Alex – Scaling his financial education platform into a full-fledged ecosystem, offering new products and reaching a global audience

Explore a New Challenge

Description	**You feel drawn to something different—whether it's a new business, career, or passion project—while applying your experience and skills.**
Questions to Ask	- Do I feel restless or unfulfilled in my current work? - Have I achieved what I set out to do, and am I ready for something new? - Is there a different way I want to create value?
Focus	Reinventing, launching something new, applying your expertise in a new domain
Benefits	- Refreshes energy and passion - Encourages personal and professional reinvention - Allows you to leverage past success in a new way
Challenges	- Can feel risky and uncertain - Requires stepping into beginner mode again - May mean letting go of what you've built
Example	Emma – Selling her successful consulting business to start an incubator that helps other entrepreneurs grow their companies

Walking the Talk

I wouldn't ask you to do this work without doing it myself.

Just as you have, I've revisited my original vision. I've looked at what's changed, what's stayed true, and what's starting to evolve in surprising ways. Writing this book has been its own transformation; stretching me, challenging me, and solidifying how powerful it is to put language around change.

So, I'm pausing here. Before rushing toward the next project or goal, I'm taking my own advice: acknowledging the work, the growth, and the learning, and letting myself feel what it means to land here.

As I reflect, I'm noticing something important:

My "why" is expanding.

The mission remains the same: to help people grow, evolve, and lead lives rooted in clarity and purpose. But how that mission comes to life may be evolving. Right now, Path #2: Scale & Expand feels most aligned.

That might look like:

- Speaking – sharing these ideas with broader audiences and helping people activate their own *Ooh* to *Ooh La La* journey.
- Coaching – guiding individuals and teams through transformation with these tools in hand.
- Creating new platforms – programs, writing, collaborations that increase the impact and broaden the reach of this work.

But I'm holding it lightly. I'm letting clarity come from action, not pressure. The path forward is unfolding, one honest step at a time.

Because if there's one truth that keeps repeating, it's this:

Transformation is an ongoing relationship, not a one-time event.

Your Turn

Maybe you're also standing at a threshold.

Not sure exactly what's next but sure that something's ready to evolve.

As you choose your next step, remember:

- You don't have to have it all figured out.
- You don't have to commit to a lifetime, just the next move.
- You don't have to follow the original script if your heart's moved somewhere new.

Trust the process. Revisit your "why." Choose the next step that feels most aligned with who you are now. This is transformation in motion.

A New Beginning

This isn't the end; it's a new beginning, a new launchpad!

This time, you're moving forward with experience, data, and confidence. You know yourself better than ever before. You understand what works for you and what doesn't. You've proven that you can push through challenges, adapt, and grow.

You've done it before. And now, you get to do it again, with more strength and direction than ever before. You got this!

OOH LA LA HIGHLIGHTS

STEP 11: REINVENT - THE JOURNEY CONTINUES

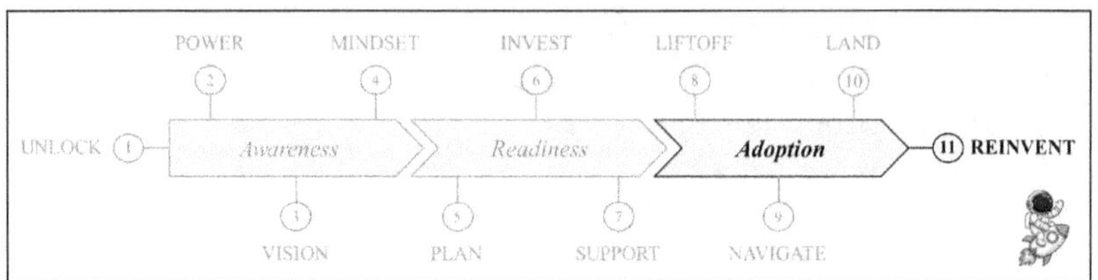

MISSION BRIEF

Success is not final; it's a launchpad for what comes next. Reaching the top of your growth curve presents a critical choice: optimize what you've built, scale your impact, or explore an entirely new challenge. Without intentional reinvention, even success can fade into stagnation or decline. The key to long-term growth is choosing your next move before the momentum slows.

CRITICAL SYSTEMS CHECK

- The *Ooh La La* Trap – Why Success Can Lead to Stagnation
    - If you don't evolve, you risk repeating past successes until they no longer work.
    - Growth slows subtly: by the time you notice, decline may have already begun.
- Step 1: Look Back – Recognizing Growth & Connecting the Dots
    - Revisit your past cycles of growth. Each phase has shaped who you are now.
    - Identify your strengths, lessons, and patterns. These hold clues for your next move.
- Step 2: Look Forward – Aligning with What's Next
    - Does your original vision still spark excitement, or has it transformed into something new?
    - Are you feeling the pull to optimize, scale, or explore a new challenge?

  - Your best next step is about aligning with who you've become.
- Choosing Your Path – Three Roads to Reinvention
  - Stay & Optimize (Marie's Evolution) – Strengthen what works, refine processes, and deepen impact.
  - Scale & Expand (Alex's Ascent) – Leverage momentum, increase reach, and build a larger platform.
  - Explore a New Challenge (Emma's Next Mission) – Reinvent with a fresh challenge, using past success as a foundation.

PILOT'S REFLECTION

1. What have your past growth cycles taught you about what drives you?
2. Which of the three paths feels most aligned with your strengths and aspirations?
3. How will you intentionally shape what comes next?

NEXT COORDINATES

You've reached a new launchpad; reinvention awaits. In the conclusion, we'll reflect on your journey and leave you with a final message to carry forward into your next bold voyage.

CONCLUSION

•

THE FINAL *OOH LA LA*

The Universe Expands as You Move Forward

You've made the journey. You launched, navigated challenges, adapted, and landed successfully. You've grown, achieved, and perhaps even surpassed what you once thought was possible. And now, standing here, you realize something profound: it's a new beginning.

If there's one thing we learn from space exploration, it's that the more we discover, the more we realize there is to explore. Every planet reached reveals new galaxies beyond. Every success unlocks new levels of potential. You didn't just complete a journey; you expanded your world.

This is the moment where many stop, satisfied with what they've built. But you? You see more ahead than ever before. And now, the question isn't, "Was this the destination?" but rather, "What comes next?"

As we learned, momentum is something you create, not something you wait for.

Keeping Your Rocket Fueled

The biggest mistake people make after reaching a big goal? They stop learning.

You've worked too hard to land here only to let stagnation creep in. The best way to keep momentum is to stay curious, to keep growing, and to surround yourself with people who challenge and inspire you.

- Never stop exploring. The most successful people are the ones who keep asking, "What else is possible?"
- Keep taking risks. Growth never happens inside your comfort zone. If something excites you but also scares you a little, it's probably worth doing.
- Give back. The more you contribute to others, the more you reinforce your growth.

The cycle of success isn't a straight path. It expands as you do, opening new possibilities along the way. So, what will you do next?

- Will you refine and deepen your impact?
- Will you scale your reach?
- Will you explore brand new territories?

Whatever you choose, know that you have everything you need.

Mission Control: Your Legacy & Impact

Every great explorer brings back knowledge. Every trailblazer leaves a map. What you've achieved is part of something bigger.

Think about the people who inspired you along the way, the books, the mentors, the moments that gave you clarity when you needed it most.

Now, you have that power. Your journey could be the exact roadmap someone else needs.

The true measure of success is what you contribute. Now that you've built something, who will you lift? How will you turn your success into something that extends beyond you?

There are many ways to share what you've learned:

- Teach – Whether it's guiding a friend, sharing insights with your team, or helping a new entrepreneur, your experience is valuable.
- Document – Write about your journey. Reflection not only solidifies your lessons but also helps others.
- Support – Invest in someone else's dream, whether through encouragement, collaboration, or direct help.

Your impact isn't measured by size but by authenticity. A small action can create a ripple. Every lesson you share can change someone's trajectory.

The Final *Ooh La La*

Somewhere out there, beyond the horizon of what you know today, your next great adventure is waiting. It's calling you forward, urging you to step on the launch pad and into the unknown once again.

But before you turn this page and move on, take a moment.

Make one promise to yourself: pick one thing, big or small, that fuels your next step. Write it down. Say it out loud. Do something today that your future self will thank you for.

And finally, thank you!

Thank you for showing up. For stepping forward. For daring to dream and act. The world is better because of people like you: people who keep going, keep growing, and keep lifting others along the way.

Now, go build what only you can.

The next step. The next planet. The next galaxy. The next universe you create.

And it all starts now.

Be *Ooh La La*... Go make it happen!

ACKNOWLEDGMENTS

Writing a book is never a solo mission, and this one certainly wasn't.

First, to my wife, Amii, and my daughter, Lauren: You are my constant source of *Ooh La La*. Your love, strength, and patience created the foundation for this book and everything I do. Thank you for believing in me, especially in the quiet moments when I doubted myself.

To my team members over the years and clients: you were the spark! Your stories, breakthroughs, and brave transformations brought the *Ooh La La* Roadmap to life long before these pages ever did. You reminded me why this work matters.

To my editors: Ashley Emma, Abby-Eve Editorial and Yoanna Stefanova, and to my alpha/beta readers: Nika Booker, Danny DeCillis, Lauren Poirot, Sarah Shabbir and Himani Sharma, thank you for challenging me to go deeper, clarify the message, and stay true to the vision. Your insight elevated this book in ways I couldn't have done alone.

To my Branding and Publishing team: Katarina Naskovski, Susie Schaefer, Fiona Serjani and Dali Sulaj: you took a vision and shaped it into something beautiful for the whole world to see. *Ooh La La* to you!

To the mentors who shaped my thinking (too many names to list, but you know who you are): thank you! I stand on the shoulders of giants in the fields of coaching, change management, and leadership.

And finally, to my readers: If this book found its way to your hands, I hope it also finds its way to your heart. Thank you for daring to dream, to change, and to say yes to your own version of *Ooh La La*.

With deep gratitude,

Raphael

INDEX: THE *OOH LA LA* SCALE

INDEX: FIGURES

GLOSSARY OF TERMS

A

- **Action:** Steps taken in the transformation process to achieve success.
- **Adoption:** The phase where action is fully embraced and momentum builds.
- **After-Action Review (AAR):** A structured reflection process to evaluate a completed mission or project, identifying what went well and areas for improvement.
- **Alignment:** Being in harmony with your values, goals, and actions.
- **Astronaut:** A person preparing for or undergoing the process of transformation. A metaphor for those going through the growth journey.
- **Authenticity:** Staying true to oneself and personal values for meaningful success.
- **Awareness:** The first phase, where one recognizes dissatisfaction and triggers change.

B

- **Belief:** Part of a mindset that shapes your decisions and actions, either empowering or limiting your progress.
- **Black Door:** A metaphor for facing fear and the unknown, leading to transformation if embraced.
- **Breakthrough:** The moment when effort results in significant progress and change.

C

- **Case for Change:** A personal manifesto that explains why transformation is necessary, aligning actions with purpose.
- **Change Management:** The structured process of managing transitions and ensuring sustainable change.
- **Coaching:** Guidance provided to help others grow and accelerate progress.

- **Commitment:** A dedicated focus to pursue a vision, turning intention into action and results.
- **Compensation:** The rewards or benefits gained from the value provided to others. Involves aligning efforts with meaningful contributions.
- **Courage:** The willingness to take risks and step into uncertainty to pursue transformation.

D

- **Direction:** The guidance or path one follows in their journey of transformation.
- **Doubt:** The uncertainty or fear that can hold one back from making progress.
- **Drive:** Internal energy to move forward and act.

E

- **Empathy:** The ability to understand and share the feelings of others, crucial for leadership.
- **Engagement:** Active participation in the transformation process and with others involved.
- **Entrepreneurship:** The act of starting and growing a business or venture, often requiring risk, innovation, and adaptability.
- **Execution:** The process of translating a plan into action; it's the phase where the strategy is put into practice and challenges are encountered.

F

- **Failure:** The natural result of attempting new things; it's a stepping stone to success, not a permanent state.
- **Fear:** A natural emotion that can hinder progress, often requiring courage to overcome.
- **Founder's Trap:** The tendency for entrepreneurs or creators to become the bottleneck in their business or mission by trying to do everything themselves, impeding growth.
- **Fulfillment:** The sense of satisfaction and joy derived from living authentically and purposefully.

G

- **Goal Setting:** The act of defining specific, measurable objectives for transformation.
- **Growth:** The process of personal and professional development over time.
- **Growth Mindset:** The belief that abilities and intelligence can be developed through dedication and work.

H

- **Honeymoon Trap:** The illusion of continuous success and momentum that often follows early wins, which can lead to overconfidence and a lack of sustained effort.

I

- **Intentionality:** The practice of acting with clear purpose and focus.
- **Intrinsic Motivation:** Internal drive fueled by purpose, rather than external rewards.

J

- **Journey:** The ongoing process of transformation, growth, and self-discovery.

K

- **Key Results:** Measurable milestones or outcomes that indicate progress toward an objective. Part of the OKR (Objectives and Key Results) system.

L

- **Lagging Indicators:** Outcomes or results that reflect past performance; often measured to confirm whether goals or objectives were achieved.
- **Leadership:** The ability to guide and inspire others through change and growth.
- **Leading Indicators:** Actions or behaviors that predict future results; often tracked to ensure progress is being made toward long-term goals.

- **Leverage:** Using available resources, strengths, or networks to accelerate progress. Leverage is key for scaling efforts.

M

- **Mastery:** The ongoing process of perfecting a skill or area of expertise.
- **Mindset:** The belief system that shapes how you respond to challenges, setbacks, and growth opportunities in pursuit of goals.
- **Mission Blueprint:** A clear, actionable plan to bridge the gap between where you are and where you want to be. It includes Objectives and Key Results (OKRs), Key Activities, and focus actions.
- **Momentum:** The force that builds as you take consistent action towards your goals.

O

- **Obstacle:** Challenges or barriers that can slow down progress or require new strategies to overcome.
- **OKRs (Objectives and Key Results):** A goal-setting framework that helps to track progress and ensure alignment with mission goals.
- **Ownership:** Taking responsibility for one's actions and outcomes in the transformation journey.

P

- **Performance Metrics:** Indicators (leading or lagging) used to track and assess progress.
- **Pit of Despair:** A phase in the transformation journey where doubts begin to set in. It's a natural part of the process that often precedes a breakthrough.
- **Progress:** The forward movement and development towards achieving goals.
- **Purpose:** The underlying reason or intention that drives one's actions and goals.

Q

- **Quick Wins:** Small, achievable successes that build momentum in the transformation process.

R

- **Readiness:** The state of being prepared and willing to act toward transformation.
- **Reinvention:** The conscious process of evolving your approach, identity, or work to stay aligned with new realities, opportunities, and challenges.
- **Resilience:** The ability to bounce back and persist through challenges and adversity.
- **Resistance:** A powerful internal force that manifests as procrastination, self-doubt, and distractions. It often appears when you're making meaningful progress.

S

- **S-Curve:** The growth trajectory representing the learning, growth, and eventual reinvention phases of a journey. Understanding your position on the S-Curve helps navigate challenges and sustain momentum.
- **Self-Awareness:** Understanding one's strengths, weaknesses, and emotional responses.
- **Success:** Achieving personal or professional goals, often defined by individual values.
- **Systems:** The organized methods and tools used to manage and track progress.

T

- **Three Feet from Gold:** The metaphor for quitting right before achieving success. It highlights the danger of giving up when progress is about to break through.
- **Transformation:** A deep, lasting change in one's life or work that aligns with personal goals.

U

- **Unlock:** The moment of realization or decision that sparks the transformation process.

V

- **Vision:** A clear and compelling picture of one's desired future or goal.
- **Values:** The principles and beliefs that guide decisions and behaviors during change.

X

- **X Factor:** A unique quality or skill that sets someone apart in their transformation journey. Often represents the one action or focus area that drives the most momentum in achieving success.

ABOUT RAPHAEL POIROT

Raphael Poirot is a transformation strategist, speaker, and leadership coach with over 25 years of experience guiding individuals, teams, and organizations through breakthrough growth and meaningful change. Known for his warm, grounded presence and sharp strategic perspective, he has helped build businesses, guide reinventions, and lead teams through complex transitions. With a passion for human potential and a knack for blending practical tools with personal wisdom, Raphael empowers people to shed doubt, embrace their unique brilliance, and take bold, confident action.

Be *Ooh La La* was born from decades of real-world experience and Raphael's conviction that the most successful people aren't necessarily the smartest or most connected; they're the ones who show up, adapt, and keep moving forward. This book is his invitation to anyone ready to break free from self-doubt and live and lead with authenticity and flair.

Originally from France, Raphael lives just outside Chicago with his wife Amii and their daughter Lauren. When he's not writing, coaching, or speaking, you'll find him in the garden, on the golf course, or sipping a perfectly crafted espresso—always with a dash of French flair and a whole lot of *Ooh La La*.

THE *OOH LA LA* CHALLENGE!

Welcome to the *Ooh La La* Challenge!

This is your opportunity to bring the excitement and inspiration of this book into the world around you! Here's how you can join in:

Step 1: Read *Be Ooh La La*

Start by diving into the pages and getting inspired by the journey. Let the ideas, lessons, and stories sink in.

Step 2: Take a Picture

Find an *Ooh La La* place, whether it's a cool spot in your city, a hidden gem you've discovered, or a beautiful place around the world. Snap a picture of your book in that location.

We want to see your adventures!

Step 3: Post on the Challenge Page

Scan the QR code to visit the challenge page, where you can submit your picture OR share it on social media using the hashtag #*Ooh*LaLaChallenge and tag us @*ooh*lala.writer

Your photo might even be featured, and some of the most creative entries will win prizes!

It's that easy! Join the movement, have some fun, and spread the *Ooh La La* energy wherever you go.

Get in Touch

We'd love to hear from you! Whether it's about the challenge, feedback on the book, or just to connect, here's how you can reach us:

- Website: www.raphaelpoirot.com
- Instagram: @*ooh*lala.writer
- Email: info@raphaelpoirot.com

www.ingramcontent.com/pod-product-compliance
Lightning Source LLC
LaVergne TN
LVHW020712110826
845149LV00012B/2228

* 9 7 9 8 9 9 3 0 8 4 1 0 7 *